Autodesk® Vault Professional 2021 Data Management for AutoCAD® Users

Learning Guide
1st Edition

Authorized Publisher

ASCENT - Center for Technical Knowledge®
Autodesk® Vault Professional 2021
Data Management for AutoCAD® Users
1st Edition

Prepared and produced by:

ASCENT Center for Technical Knowledge
630 Peter Jefferson Parkway, Suite 175
Charlottesville, VA 22911

866-527-2368
www.ASCENTed.com

Lead Contributor: Barb Nash

ASCENT - Center for Technical Knowledge (a division of Rand Worldwide Inc.) is a leading developer of professional learning materials and knowledge products for engineering software applications. ASCENT specializes in designing targeted content that facilitates application-based learning with hands-on software experience. For over 25 years, ASCENT has helped users become more productive through tailored custom learning solutions.

We welcome any comments you may have regarding this guide, or any of our products. To contact us please email: feedback@ASCENTed.com.

Contents

Preface

The *Autodesk® Vault Professional 2021: Data Management for AutoCAD® Users* guide introduces the Autodesk Vault Professional 2021 software to AutoCAD users. This guide is intended for AutoCAD users who need to access their design files from the Autodesk Vault software. It provides an introduction to the Autodesk Vault Professional software and focuses on Autodesk Vault's features for managing design projects with the AutoCAD software from a user's perspective.

You can use the Autodesk Vault Professional 2021 software and should use the AutoCAD 2021 software to complete the exercises in this guide. Note that this guide does not cover administrative functionality. Hands-on exercises are included to reinforce how to manage the design workflow process using the Autodesk Vault Professional software. Included with this guide is a training Vault that can be used alongside a production Vault, to ensure that both Vaults can be accessed from the Autodesk Vault software.

Topics Covered

- Introduction to Autodesk Vault features
- Using the Autodesk Vault client
- Searching the Vault
- Working with non-CAD files in the Vault
- Working with AutoCAD files including XREFs in the Vault
- Customizing the user interface
- Data management and reusing design data

Prerequisites

- Access to the 2021.0 version of the software, to ensure compatibility with this guide. Future software updates that are released by Autodesk may include changes that are not reflected in this guide. The practices and files included with this guide might not be compatible with prior versions (e.g., 2020).
- Good working knowledge of the AutoCAD software.

Note on Software Setup

This guide assumes a standard installation of the software using the default preferences during installation. Lectures and practices use the standard software templates and default options for the Content Libraries.

Students and Educators Can Access Free Autodesk Software and Resources

Autodesk challenges you to get started with free educational licenses for professional software and creativity apps used by millions of architects, engineers, designers, and hobbyists today. Bring Autodesk software into your classroom, studio, or workshop to learn, teach, and explore real-world design challenges the way professionals do.

Get started today - register at the Autodesk Education Community and download one of the many Autodesk software applications available.

Visit www.autodesk.com/education/home/

Note: Free products are subject to the terms and conditions of the end-user license and services agreement that accompanies the software. The software is for personal use for education purposes and is not intended for classroom or lab use.

Lead Contributor: Barb Nash

With extensive experience in project management and eLearning development, Barb's primary responsibilities include the design, development, and project management of courseware for Product Lifecycle Management (PLM) products such as Autodesk Vault and Autodesk Fusion Lifecycle. Her work also involves the development of custom training that is designed and configured to a company's specific environment, processes, and roles.

Prior to joining ASCENT in 2005, Barb managed a technical support team for 10 years supporting CAD and PDM/PLM software.

Barb is a Professional Engineer and holds a degree in Aerospace Engineering. She is also a certified Project Management Professional (PMP) and trained in Instructional Design.

Barb Nash has been the Lead Contributor for *Autodesk Vault Professional: Data Management for AutoCAD Users* since its initial release in 2019.

In This Guide

The following highlights the key features of this guide.

Feature	Description
Practice Files	The Practice Files page includes a link to the practice files and instructions on how to download and install them. The practice files are required to complete the practices in this guide.
Chapters	A chapter consists of the following - Learning Objectives, Instructional Content, Practices, Chapter Review Questions, and Command Summary. • **Learning Objectives** define the skills you can acquire by learning the content provided in the chapter. • **Instructional Content**, which begins right after Learning Objectives, refers to the descriptive and procedural information related to various topics. Each main topic introduces a product feature, discusses various aspects of that feature, and provides step-by-step procedures on how to use that feature. Where relevant, examples, figures, helpful hints, and notes are provided. • **Practice** for a topic follows the instructional content. Practices enable you to use the software to perform a hands-on review of a topic. It is required that you download the practice files (using the link found on the Practice Files page) prior to starting the first practice. • **Chapter Review Questions**, located close to the end of a chapter, enable you to test your knowledge of the key concepts discussed in the chapter. • **Command Summary** concludes a chapter. It contains a list of the software commands that are used throughout the chapter and provides information on where the command can be found in the software.

Practice Files

To download the practice files for this guide, use the following steps:

1. Type the URL *exactly as shown below* into the address bar of your Internet browser, to access the Course File Download page.

   Note: If you are using the ebook, you do not have to type the URL. Instead, you can access the page simply by clicking the URL below.

   ## https://www.ascented.com/getfile/id/aethiops

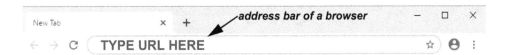

2. On the Course File Download page, click the **DOWNLOAD NOW** button, as shown below, to download the .ZIP file that contains the practice files.

3. Once the download is complete, unzip the file and extract its contents.

   The recommended practice files folder location is:
   C:\Vault Data Management Practice Files

   Note: It is recommended that you do not change the location of the practice files folder. Doing so may cause errors when completing the practices.

Stay Informed!

To receive information about upcoming events, promotional offers, and complimentary webcasts, visit:

www.ASCENTed.com/updates

Software Setup

Attach the Database

1. From the Start menu, select **Autodesk>Autodesk Data Management>
   Autodesk Data Management Server Console 2021**.

2. Log in as **Administrator** without a password.

3. Select **Vaults**, as shown below:

4. Select **Actions>Attach>***Advanced* tab to attach the Vault. Fill in the following
   details, as follows:

   • **Data File**: *C:\Program Files(86)\Microsoft SQL Server\MSSQL14.
     AUTODESKVAULT\MSSQL\DATA\Vault_Training.mdf*
     or
     *C:\Program Files\Microsoft SQL Server\MSSQL14.AUTODESKVAULT\
     MSSQL\DATA\Vault_Training.mdf*
   • **Log File**: Filled in automatically
   • **File Store**: *C:\Vault Data Management Practice Files\Vault_Training*
   • **Vault Name**: Filled in automatically

5. Click **OK**. The Attach Progress dialog box opens.

6. In the Autodesk Data Management Server Console dialog box, click **OK** when
   prompted that the vault was attached successfully.

7. Select the **Vault_Training** vault.

8. Select **Actions>Content Indexing Service**.

9. In the Content Indexing Service dialog box, select **Yes, enable the Content
   Indexing Service**.

---

10. Click **OK**.

11. Remain in the Autodesk Data Management Server Console to create users.

Set Up Users

1. If the Autodesk Data Management Server Console is not open, from the Start menu, select **Autodesk>Autodesk Data Management>Autodesk Data Management Server Console 2021** and log in as Administrator. No password is required. Select **Tools>Administration** and select the *Security* tab.

2. Click **Manage Users...**.

3. Click **New User**.

4. Set the *First Name* to **user1**.

5. Set the *User Name* to **user1**. Do not enter a password.

6. Click **Roles...** and select **Administrator, Document Editor (Level 2), Change Order Editor (Level 2), and Item Editor (Level 2)**. Click **OK**.

7. Click **Vaults...** and select **Vault_Training**. Click **OK**. The New User dialog box should display as shown below.

8. Click **OK**.

9. Create other users with a *User Name* of **user2** using the same roles and vault as defined for user1.

10. Click **OK**. Close the dialog boxes.

11. Close the Autodesk Data Management Server Console.

12. Log in to Autodesk Vault client, **Vault_Training** vault as Administrator, no password.

13. Select **Tools>Administration>Global Settings**.

14. Select the *Change Orders* tab and then click **Define**. In the Routing window, click **Edit** to edit the Default Routing. Select **user1** and add all of the available roles to **user1**, as shown below.

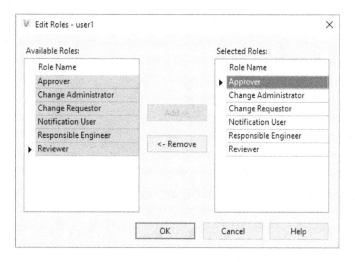

15. Close the dialog boxes.

Set Up Duplicate Search (for Inventor files only)

1. Select **Tools>Administration>Global Settings**. In the *Integrations* tab, select the **Enable Job Server** option and click **Close**.

2. Select **Tools>Administration>Vault Settings**.

3. In the *Files* tab, click **Configure...** in the Duplicate Search Settings section, as shown below.

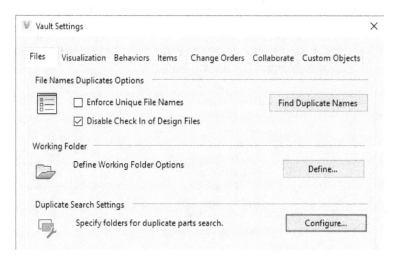

4. Ensure the **Enable Duplicate Search** option is selected.

5. Click ✚ and select the $ folder, then click **OK** to start indexing.

6. Close the Vault Settings dialog box.

Chapter

1

Introduction to Autodesk Vault

Autodesk® Vault is Product Lifecycle Management software (PLM) that enables you to secure, consolidate, and organize all product information for easy reference, sharing, and reuse. Autodesk Vault users can store and search both non-CAD data (such as Microsoft® Word and Microsoft® Excel® files) and CAD data (such as Autodesk® Inventor®, AutoCAD®, and DWF files). In this chapter, you learn about the features in the Autodesk Vault software to manage your AutoCAD designs.

Learning Objectives in This Chapter

- Describe the key features and benefits of the Autodesk Vault software.
- Differentiate between terms used in the Autodesk Vault software.
- Identify the ways that Autodesk Vault functions can be accessed.

1.1 Autodesk Vault Features

Autodesk Vault is Product Lifecycle Management (PLM) software that manages the life of a design from conception to retirement. The files associated with the design are tracked and managed. The software also manages who is permitted to work with files at specific times.

The Autodesk Vault software's capabilities include:

- Central repository for data.

- Security access control to data.

- Protection against accidentally overwriting design data.

- Object relationship management.

- Tracks revision history.

- Search and view tools to easily find and view design data.

- Manages CAD and non-CAD data.

- Direct CAD Integration with Autodesk CAD products: Autodesk Inventor, AutoCAD, AutoCAD Mechanical, Autodesk Civil 3D®, and many more.

- Copy Design tool for copying an entire design, including all related files, and maintaining their relationships to each other in the new design.

- Change Management functionality.

- Items/Bill of Materials Management.

This learning guide focuses on the core functionality of the Autodesk Vault Professional software from a user's perspective.

1.2 Terms and Definitions

Before working with the software, it is recommended to become familiar with the fundamental terminology of the Autodesk Vault software. This section describes some of the commonly used Autodesk Vault terminology.

Object

Object is a generic term used to describe anything stored in the Autodesk Vault database, such as files and items.

File

File is the term used to describe files stored in the Autodesk Vault database. The vault can store any type of file, including Autodesk Inventor, Project files, AutoCAD, AutoCAD Mechanical, Autodesk Civil 3D, Microsoft Excel, Microsoft Word, etc.

By default, files stored in the Autodesk Vault database do not require unique filenames. Select **Tools>Administration>Vault Settings** and select **Enforce Unique File Names** to ensure that the filenames are unique in the Autodesk Vault software, as shown in Figure 1–1.

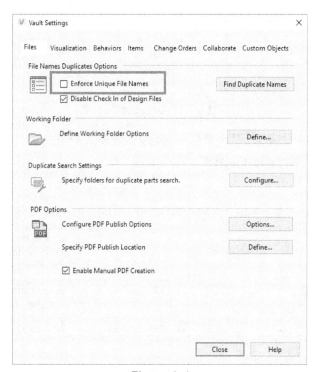

Figure 1–1

> **Best Practice: Using Unique Filenames**
>
> Enforcing unique filenames is a recommended best practice. If not previously enforced, you can search for duplicates by clicking **Find Duplicates**.

Item

An Item is an object type that represents all information related to the end item part. It is a container for data that can include CAD files (and other associated reference files), ECOs, and BOMs. Items refer to what a company manages, assembles, sells, and manufactures. An item is identified by its item number or part number. Not only can items represent parts and assemblies, they can also represent paint, lubricants, etc.

Change Order

A Change Order, also referred to as an ECO, is an object that describes why, how, and when changes are made to an Item and/or a CAD file. The result and purpose of a Change Order is to release these objects.

Properties/ Metadata

Object properties refer to the information or metadata associated with a specific object in the Autodesk Vault database. Every object in the database has properties that include the object name, state, revision, version, and other attributes. Since the Autodesk Vault software stores these properties in the database, they can be searched for to locate an object.

File Management Terminology

Autodesk Vault's operations include recording the process of change in a file. The terminology related to these processes is described as follows:

Term	Description
Get	Downloads a copy of a file from the vault into a client's working folder. This option enables you to either get a read-only copy of the files, or mark the file as being worked on (checked out) so that you can make modifications. The Autodesk Vault software always contains the master copy of the file.
Check Out	Marks the file as being worked on (checked out) but does not download a copy to your working folder.
Undo Check Out	Checks the selected files back in, unmodified, without creating a new version and without uploading the files back to the vault.

Check In	Uploads a file from the client's working folder to the Autodesk Vault database. You are prompted to save a file before check in if you have not already done so.
Open	Opens the latest version of a file in the associated application. It downloads a copy of the file from the vault into a client's working folder.
Version	Defines the state of the file in the change process. It is an incremental numeric attribute that changes every time a file is changed and submitted (checked in) to the database.
Working Copy	A local copy of the file that has been downloaded from the vault and is located in a local directory or workspace on your machine. The downloading takes place during **Get** and **Open** operations.
File Status in Vault (Vault Status)	Defined by both the state of the file (checked in, checked out, etc.) and the state of the file in the vault compared to the local copy on the client's file system (newer, older, etc.).
Refresh	Updates the current state of the files in the vault.
Revision	Defines a collection of versions with a single character typically, such as A or B. A revision is created with the **Revise** command. Revisions can also be automatically generated through a Lifecycle State change.

Best Practice: Delete Working Copies

The vault contains all of the master files, which means you are working on a copy of the master file each time you check it out. When you check a file back into the Vault, it becomes the latest version of the master file. Consider your workspace or local working folders as a temporary location for your design files as they are being modified. A recommended best practice is to delete the working copies when you check them in.

Category

Categories are used to group objects and help to assign behaviors and rules to each group of objects. A category can automatically assign user-defined properties to objects in the Vault. Categories can also be used to automatically assign lifecycle definitions or revision values to files.

Lifecycle

Lifecycles are used to manage the stages of maturity of an object. Objects such as files, items and change orders move from state to state (e.g., Work in Progress > For Review > Released, etc.), as managed by the lifecycle definition. At each lifecycle state, an individual is responsible for performing some type of work. An example of a file or item lifecycle is shown in Figure 1–2. An example of a change order object or ECO lifecycle is shown in Figure 1–3.

File or Item Lifecycle Example

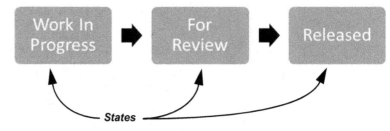

Figure 1–2

ECO (Change Order) Lifecycle Example

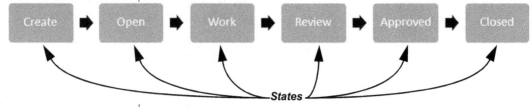

Figure 1–3

1.3 Accessing Autodesk Vault

There are two ways of accessing Autodesk Vault functions:

* Logging in to the Autodesk Vault client.

* Logging in from AutoCAD to use the AutoCAD Vault Add-in.

Autodesk Vault Client

The Autodesk Vault client (also referred to as Autodesk Vault Explorer), provides the user interface for accessing data in the vault. Tasks performed in the Autodesk Vault client software include searching the vault, viewing file status and history, and checking files in and out. The Autodesk Vault software can also be launched and accessed from the AutoCAD software.

The Autodesk Vault client software displays a complete view of the data in the vault. The main window includes the Navigation pane, Main table, Preview pane, and Properties grid, as shown in Figure 1–4.

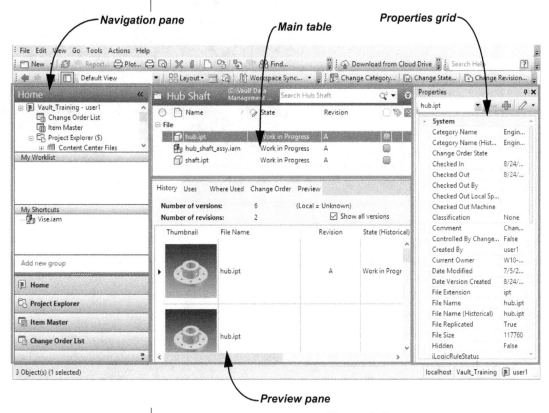

Figure 1–4

AutoCAD Vault Add-in

The AutoCAD software has a direct integration with Autodesk Vault using the AutoCAD Vault Add-in. This means that the AutoCAD software has a Vault menu or tab in its interface, providing quick access to the Autodesk Vault options. Vault options are also available through the External References palette within AutoCAD. File operations, such as Check In and Check Out, can be performed from within the AutoCAD interface to maintain file relationship integrity. The integration interface showing the Vault menu is as shown in Figure 1–5.

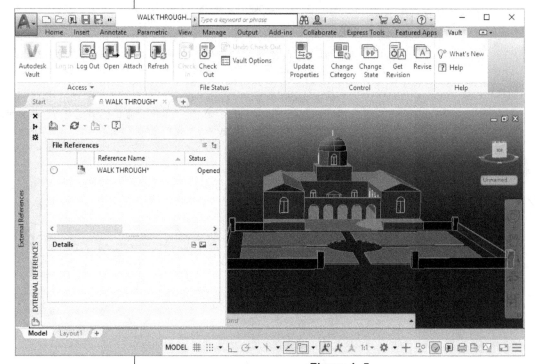

Figure 1–5

Autodesk Inventor Vault Add-in

The Autodesk Inventor software has a direct integration with Autodesk Vault using the Autodesk Inventor Vault Add-in. This means that the Autodesk Inventor software has a Vault menu or tab in its interface, providing quick access to the Autodesk Vault options. File operations, such as Check In and Check Out, can be performed from within the Autodesk Inventor interface to maintain file relationship integrity. The integration interface showing the Vault menu is shown in Figure 1–6.

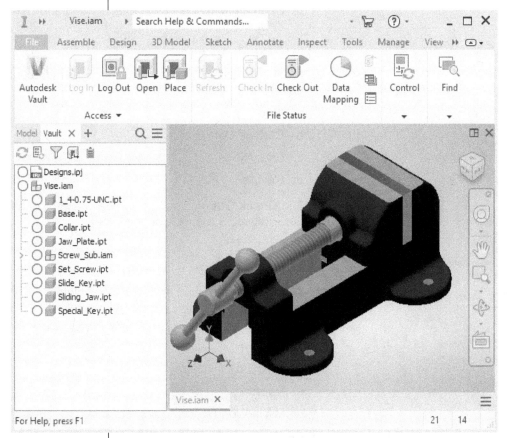

Figure 1–6

Chapter Review Questions

1. What are some of the key features and benefits of the Autodesk Vault software?

   a. Central repository for data.

   b. Protection against accidentally overwriting design data.

   c. Search and display tools to easily find and view design data.

   d. All of the above.

2. What term is used to describe the stages of maturity of an object?

   a. Item

   b. Change Order

   c. Lifecycle

   d. Revision

3. The **Check Out** command downloads a copy of a file from the vault into a client's working folder.

   a. True

   b. False

4. Which of the following provides a complete view of all of the data files in the vault?

   a. Autodesk Vault Client (also known as Autodesk Vault Explorer)

   b. AutoCAD

   c. Inventor

   d. Vault Add-in

5. What term relates to the incremental numeric attribute that changes every time a file is changed, submitted, and checked in to the database?

   a. State

   b. Revision

   c. Version

   d. File Status

6. In Figure 1–7, what is the name of the highlighted area?

   a. Navigation pane

   b. Preview pane

   c. Main table

   d. Properties grid

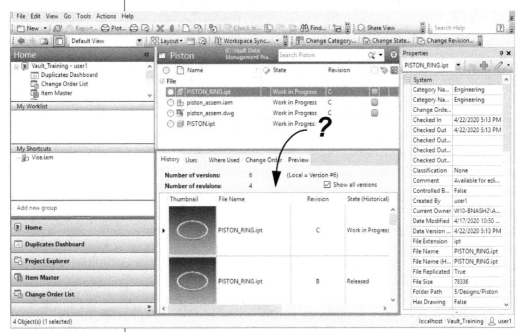

Figure 1–7

Orientation to Autodesk Vault

This chapter takes you through the process of logging in to the Autodesk® Vault client software, setting up the vault folder structure, familiarizing yourself with the interface and accessing data, and then adding non-CAD files to the vault.

Learning Objectives in This Chapter

- Log in to the Autodesk Vault client.
- Set the vault working folder.
- Set up the vault folder structure in the Autodesk Vault software.
- Differentiate between the main areas of the Autodesk Vault interface.
- Describe the functions of each main area of the Autodesk Vault interface.
- Add non-CAD files to the Autodesk Vault software using the **Add Files** command and the drag-and-drop method.

2.1 Logging In to the Autodesk Vault Client

Use the following steps to log in to the Autodesk Vault client software. Once logged in, you have access to the metadata and physical files.

How To: Log In to the Autodesk Vault Client

1. The Autodesk Vault client can be started using one of the following methods:

   - Double-click on 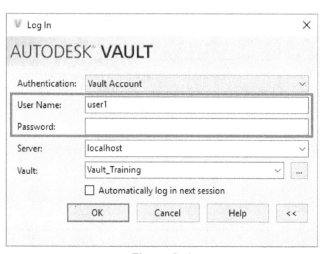 (Autodesk Vault Professional 2020) on the desktop.
   - Select **Autodesk Data Management>Autodesk Vault Professional 2021** from the **Start** menu.
   - Select **Autodesk Vault Professional 2021** in the desktop Apps list.

2. In the Log In dialog box, enter the *User Name* and *Password* as shown in Figure 2–1.

Figure 2–1

3. In the Server drop-down list, select the server, as required.
4. In the Vault drop-down list, select the vault, as required. You can also click ⌷ (Browse) to display the list of active vaults.
5. Select **Automatically Log in next session**. In subsequent sessions, this enables you to be automatically logged into the vault as the previous specified user.
6. Click **OK**.

2.2 Folder Structure

After logging in to the Autodesk Vault client for the first time, you should familiarize yourself with the vault folder structure and associated client folders in the Navigation pane.

Vault Folders

The Root in the Autodesk Vault client (also known as the Project Explorer Root) is the top-level directory and is defined as $. Typically, a *Designs* folder or project folders are created below the Root to hold all of your designs. Library folders contain read-only library parts and require their own folder structure, separate from the *Designs* folder structure. They must also be located directly below the Root.

Working Folder

The working folder is a location on the client machine to which design files are copied when they have been either copied as read-only or checked out of the database using the **Get** command.

The working folder is set for the Root of the vault and not for each folder. This is because the folder structure used in the vault is automatically replicated below the working folder on the client's machine when using the **Get** command. When the Autodesk Vault client software is installed, a working folder is defined by default so that you can begin working with a vault. The default working folder is *My Documents>Vault*.

A new working folder can be defined if a consistent working folder for all users has not been enforced by the system administrator. If the administrator has enforced a consistent working folder, a warning message opens indicating that the working folder cannot be changed if you try to set a new one.

By default, the working folder path is not displayed in the title bar. To display the path, select **Tools>Options** and select the **Show working folder location** option.

> ### Best Practice: Store Files Temporarily in Working Folder
>
> As a recommended best practice, the working folder should be considered a temporary folder in which to store files until they are checked back into the vault. Once checked back into the vault, the files should be deleted.

How To: Set Up the Vault Folder Structure

1. Set the working folder if it has not already been enforced by the system administrator. To set the working folder, select the root of the vault and select **File>Set Working Folder**, as shown in Figure 2–2.

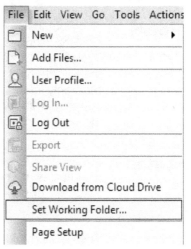

Figure 2–2

A working folder is set up for each user, machine, and vault.

2. Browse to the folder on your machine that is at the top-level directory of all of your design folders. Click **OK** when the design folder is selected. If the folder does not exist, you can create one by clicking **Make New Folder**.

3. Create the top-level design folder if it has not already been created. Select the Project Explorer Root, right-click on it, and select **New Folder**, as shown in Figure 2–3.

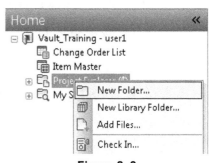

Figure 2–3

You can create as many subfolders for each design as required. If a folder hierarchy does exist on the local machine, the folder hierarchy in the vault should match for simplicity. However, if vault folders do not have a match on the local machine, the folder structure on the local machine is replicated to match the vault folder structure, as required, when using the **Get** command.

Similarly, if the *Designs* local folder structure contains additional subfolders in preparation for adding designs to the vault, these subfolders are automatically created (as required) in the vault as files are added. When you have created the required folders, you might need to make corrections or modifications to the folder structure, such as renaming or deleting folders.

- To rename a folder, right-click on it and select **Rename**.

- To delete a folder, right-click on it and select **Delete**.

4. Create the top-level library folder if it has not already been created. Select the Vault Explorer Root, right-click, and select **New Library Folder**, as shown in Figure 2–4.

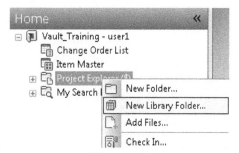

Figure 2–4

Links

Links can be created anywhere in the Project Explorer and point to a target object (such as a file, folder, item, or change order). The target object resides in one location only. Organizing objects and links in a project folder can facilitate management and reporting. Commands such as **Check Out** and **Check In** can be performed using a link and are executed on the target object. Note that the **Delete** and **Move** commands only affect the link and not the target object.

How To: Create a Link

1. Select the target object for the link.
2. In the Edit menu, select **Copy** as shown in Figure 2–5.

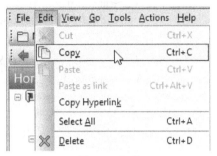

Figure 2–5

3. Select the link's destination folder.
4. In the Edit menu, select **Paste as link** as shown in Figure 2–6.

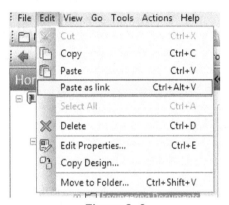

Figure 2–6

5. The link is created in that folder with an arrow included in the entity icon as shown in Figure 2–7.

Figure 2–7

2.3 Autodesk Vault Interface Overview

The Autodesk Vault interface consists of the following main areas, as shown in Figure 2–8:

- Navigation pane

- Main table or pane

- Preview pane

- Properties grid

- Toolbars

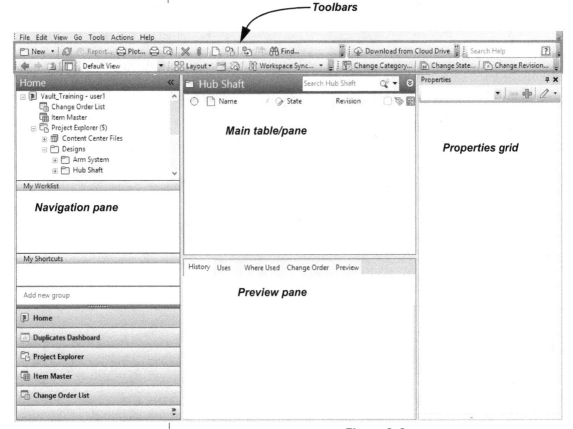

Figure 2–8

The Navigation pane shows the folder structure in a tree format, while the data displays in the Main and Preview panes in a column or grid format. An example is shown in Figure 2–9.

Navigation pane   *Main table/pane*   *Properties grid*

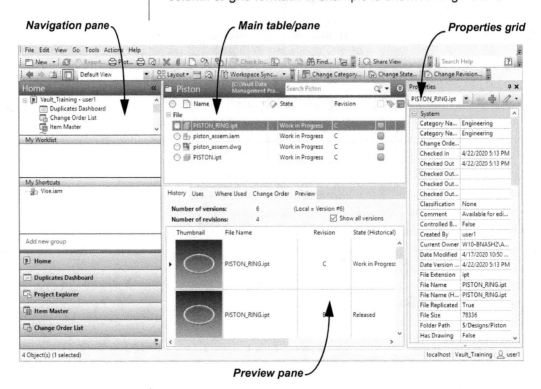

Preview pane

Figure 2–9

2.4 Navigation Pane

The Navigation pane, located on the left side of the interface, contains the *Home*, *Duplicates Dashboard*, *Project Explorer*, *Item Master,* and *Change Order List* tabs. The active tab is highlighted in orange. The Duplicates Dashboard, Project Explorer, Item Master, and Change Order List data can be accessed by clicking on their respective links, or from the *Home* tab, as shown in Figure 2–10.

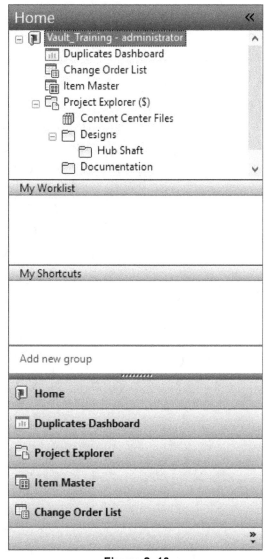

Figure 2–10

The Project Explorer displays the vault objects in a tree view, as shown in Figure 2–11.

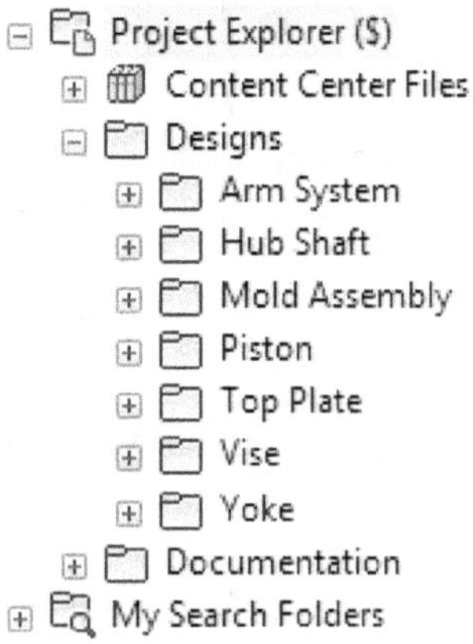

```
⊟ 🗗 Project Explorer ($)
    ⊞ 🎯 Content Center Files
    ⊟ 🗀 Designs
        ⊞ 🗀 Arm System
        ⊞ 🗀 Hub Shaft
        ⊞ 🗀 Mold Assembly
        ⊞ 🗀 Piston
        ⊞ 🗀 Top Plate
        ⊞ 🗀 Vise
        ⊞ 🗀 Yoke
    ⊞ 🗀 Documentation
⊞ 🗗 My Search Folders
```

Figure 2–11

Folders with subfolders display ⊞ (Expand) next to each folder name, which you can click to expand the branch. Expanded folders display ⊟ (Collapse), which enables you to collapse the branch when clicked. Right-click on a folder to display the contextual options.

The Project Explorer also contains a folder called *My Search Folders*. You can use this to create saved searches for quick access.

2.5 Main Table

The Main table or pane display changes depending on the tab you are using:

- Using the *Project Explorer* tab, it displays objects that reside in the selected vault folder.

- Using the *Item Master* tab, it displays the Item Master list.

- Using the *Change Order List* tab, it displays the Change Order objects.

- Using the *Duplicates Dashboard* tab, it displays the Duplicate Parts Overview and Indexed Data Overview.

Project Explorer

When using the Project Explorer, the vault folder name displays in the Main table title bar. To display the working folder path name instead of just the folder names used, select **Tools>Options** and select **Show working folder location**. The Main table displaying files and the local working folder path is shown in Figure 2–12.

Displays the vault folder name and the path to the folder

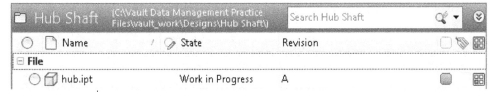

Figure 2–12

The default columns that display include: *Vault Status*, *Entity Icon*, *Name*, *State*, *Revision*, *Category Glyph*, *Property Compliance*, and *Linked to Item*.

It is a best practice to keep the DWF files hidden. If they display during checkout, they are also checked out.

By default, automatically generated .DWF files are hidden in the list. To display the .DWF file, select **Tools>Options** and then select **Show hidden files** in the Options dialog box.

You can customize the columns in the Main table to show, remove, reorder, and sort additional file properties as required by right-clicking on a column header and using the **Customize View>Fields** option.

Item Master

If the *Item Master* tab is selected, the Main table displays the items in the table. The default columns that display include: *Vault Status, Number, Revision, State, Title (Item, CO), File Link State, Category Glyph, Property Compliance,* and *Controlled by Change Order,* as shown in Figure 2–13.

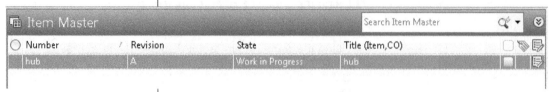

Figure 2–13

Change Order List

If the *Change Order List* tab is selected, the main table displays the Change Order objects in the table. The default columns that display include: *Vault Status, Number of File Attachments, Number, State, Title (Item, CO),* and *Due Date,* as shown in Figure 2–14.

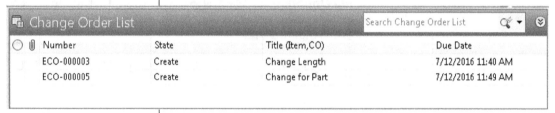

Figure 2–14

Duplicates Dashboard

If the *Duplicates Dashboard* tab is selected, the main table displays the Duplicate Parts Overview and Indexed Data Overview, as shown in Figure 2–15.

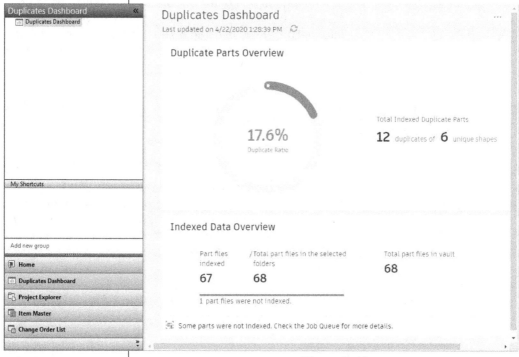

Figure 2–15

2.6 Preview Pane

The Preview pane is one of three main areas in the Autodesk Vault interface (the other two are the Navigation pane and the Main table). When a file is selected, the Preview pane displays information, which is categorized into tabs. These tabs are different for the Project Explorer, Item Master, and Change Order list.

Project Explorer

When using the Project Explorer, the tabs are: *History*, *Uses*, *Where Used*, and *Preview*.

History Tab

The *History* tab displays versions of the file that has been selected in the Main table. File properties display for each version. The default properties displayed include the *Thumbnail*, *File Name*, *Version*, *Created By* (which user checked in the file), *Checked In* (date of the version), and *Comment*, as shown in Figure 2–16.

History	Uses	Where Used	Change Order	Preview			
Number of versions:	2		(Local = Version #2)				
Number of revisions:	1						☑ Show all versions

Thumbnail	File Name	Version	Created By	Checke...	Comment
	Office.dwg	2	Administrator	10/8/20...	Removed elevation
	Office.dwg	1	Administrator	10/8/20...	Initial submission

Figure 2–16

You can customize the columns to show, remove, reorder, and sort additional file properties as required by right-clicking on a column header and using the **Customize View>Fields** option.

Uses Tab

The *Uses* tab lists all of the files used in the selected file as shown in Figure 2–17. The Revision drop-down list enables you to see files that were used throughout the history of the selected file.

Figure 2–17

Where Used Tab

The *Where Used* tab displays files in the vault that reference the selected file, as shown in Figure 2–18.

Figure 2–18

Click 🛈 (Parents Loaded) to display the Direct and Total number of parents loaded. Use the Revision drop-down list to display where the selected file has been used throughout its history.

Preview Tab

The *Preview* tab displays a carousel view of the selected file, as shown in Figure 2–19. The carousel view enables you to view thumbnails of the selected file and cycle through previous versions of the file in Vault Basic, or previous revisions and versions of the file in Vault Workgroup or Vault Professional. The file version or revision displays at the top of each thumbnail, and the last check-in date displays at the bottom.

Figure 2–19

For files (such as parts, assemblies, and Autodesk Inventor drawings), Autodesk Vault attaches a visualization file to the selected file. When the thumbnail is selected, the associated visualization file is loaded using the Autodesk DWF Viewer (.IPT, .IAM, or .IDW) or a document previewer (.DOC, .XLS, .PPT, .XPS, .CSV, or .ZIP). The .DWF file can be automatically generated for Autodesk Inventor models. When you select a previous version of a file a warning displays, as shown in Figure 2–20.

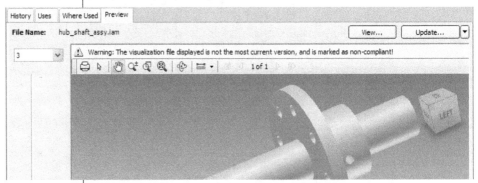

Figure 2–20

The DWF Viewer enables you to rotate, zoom, pan, print, and measure .DWF images. Use the version slider to display the history of the file.

The following DWF Viewer icons display in the Preview pane> *Preview* tab:

Icon	Description
🖐	**Pan the Canvas:** Enables you to move around the model.
Q±	**Zoom In/Out:** Enables you to zoom in or out of the model.
🔍	**Zoom Area:** Enables you to use a selection window to zoom to a specific area in the Preview window.
🔍	**Fit to Window:** Enables you to fit the model into the Preview window.
⟳	**Orbit:** Enables you to rotate the model.
▭	**Measure Length:** Enables you to measure objects on the model.

Non-DWF documents can also be previewed, including the following file formats:

- Microsoft® Office Word (.DOC, .DOCX, .DOT, .DOTX, and .RTF)
- Microsoft® Office Excel® (.XLS, .XLSB, .XLSX, and .XLTX)
- Microsoft® Office PowerPoint® (.POT, .POTX, .PPS, .PPSX, .PPT, and .PPTX)
- Microsoft® Outlook® Email previewer (*.msg)
- PDF preview handler (.PDF)
- XPS viewer (.XPS)
- Comma separated values (.CSV)
- Compressed files (.ZIP)

To control which application will be used as the default viewer for the various file formats, select **Tools>Options** and click **Document Previewers...**.

For files that cannot be viewed with the DWF Viewer or a document viewer, right-click and select **Open**, select **File>Open**, or click **Open** in the Preview pane to launch the associated application and display the file.

Item Master

For *Item Master*, the tabs are: *General, History, Bill of Materials, Where Used, Change Order,* and *View*.

Additional details will be covered in the Items and Bill of Materials Management chapter.

Change Order List

For *Change Order List*, the tabs are: *General, Records, Comments, Files, Routing,* and *Status*.

Additional details will be covered in the Change Management chapter.

2.7 Properties Grid

You can display Properties in the Properties Grid, as shown in Figure 2–21.

Figure 2–21

To manage file properties, select **Tools>Administration>Vault Settings**, and then in the *Behaviors* tab, click **Properties**. The Property Definitions dialog box opens, as shown in Figure 2–22.

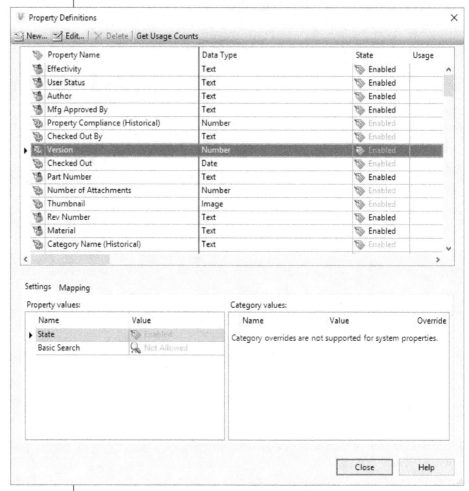

Figure 2–22

2.8 Toolbars

Autodesk Vault's standard and advanced toolbars, shown in Figure 2–23, provide fast access to many vault operations.

Standard toolbar

Advanced toolbar

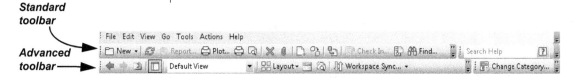

Figure 2–23

The icons available depend on the files selected in the Main table.

Standard Toolbar Icons

Icon	Description
New ▾	**New Folder** or **New Library Folder:** Creates a new folder or new library area.
⟳	**Refresh:** Updates the current state of the files in the vault.
Report...	**Report:** Create report using selected template.
Plot...	**Plot:** Plots selected files.
🖶	**Print Direct:** Prints directly to the printer.
🔍	**Print Preview:** Previews the output before it is printed.
✕	**Delete:** Deletes the selected files.
📎	**Attachments:** Select a file and view its attachment or attach additional files, as required.
📄	**Add Files:** Adds files to the vault.
📑	**Copy Design:** Copies an entire design, including all of the related files, parts, drawings, subassemblies, and attachments to a new design.
Check In...	**Check In:** Checks in the selected files.
📥	**Get:** Downloads the selected files from the vault to the working folder and are read only by default.
📤	**Undo Check Out:** Undoes the **Check Out** operation on selected files.

🔍 Find…	**Find:** Searches the vault by entering a specified text string.
🖼	**Autodesk App Store Manager:** Launches the Autodesk App Store Manager to view and manage your Autodesk Apps.

Advanced Toolbar Icons

Icon	Description
⬅	**Move Backward:** Moves you back to the previously selected folder in the Navigation pane.
➡	**Move Forward:** After moving backwards, click to return to the folder in which you started.
⬆	**Up One Level:** Moves you back to the parent of the selected folder in the Navigation pane.
▢	**Preview Pane:** Toggles the Preview pane on and off.
Default View ▼	Controls whether the default view or a custom view is assigned to control the display of the Main Table.
⊞ Layout ▾	**Layout:** Controls the display of files in the Main Table. Options include **Detail View**, **Small Icons**, or **Large Icons**.
▤	**Group By Box:** Groups column headings.
🔍	**Auto Preview:** Displays comments for each file on a separate line below the file details.
↕ Workspace Sync… ▾	**Workspace Sync:** Synchronizes the contents of your local workspace with the contents of the corresponding Vault folders.
🖩 Change Category…	**Change Category:** Changes the category of the selected object.
Change State…	**Change State:** Changes the state of the selected object.
Change Revision…	**Change Revision:** Changes the Revision of the selected object.

2.9 Adding Non-CAD Files to the Vault

You can add any file format to a vault. When a file is added, it is transferred to the vault and becomes the master file.

Your user role must be defined as Editor or Administrator to add files to the vault.

If CAD files are added using the Autodesk Vault interface, the relationship between Autodesk Inventor files, or the relationship between a DWG host file and its XREFs are not tracked. Instead, the respective Vault Add-in software should be used for this purpose.

- You can use Vault Explorer for non-CAD files.

How To: Add a Non-CAD File to the Vault

You can also drag and drop files from File Explorer to the Autodesk Vault software to add non-CAD files to the vault.

1. Select the vault folder in which you want the file to be stored.
2. Right-click and select **Add Files**.
3. Navigate to the folder in which the file is located and select the file. Click **Open**.
4. In the Add Files dialog box, select **Keep files checked out** if you want to check the file out immediately after you check it in. For example, you could use this option at the end of the work day. This ensures that the modified file is in the vault for backup and is available for viewing, but remains checked out so that you can continue with the modifications. This prevents others from checking out and changing the file.
5. Select **Delete working copies** to delete the file from your computer. This is a recommended best practice if you have finished modifying the file. When you need to modify it again or to view the file, you can retrieve it from the vault to ensure you are working with the latest.
6. In the *Enter comments to include...* area, type a description of the file, such as **Initial submission to vault**.
7. Click **OK** add the file to the vault.

Once added to the vault, the file displays in the Main table. The *Vault Status* column indicates that the file is available for check out. If the local copy was deleted, the column indicates that you do not have a local copy.

Practice 2a

Orientation to Autodesk Vault

Practice Objectives

- Log in to the Autodesk Vault software and set a working folder.
- Compare the working folder structure to the vault folder structure.
- View and analyze vaulted files.

In this practice, you will log in to the Autodesk Vault software and become familiar with the user interface. You will also set a working folder and compare the folder structure on the local machine to the vault folder structure.

Task 1 - Log in to the Autodesk Vault software.

1. Log in to the Autodesk Vault software using one of the following methods:

   - Double-click on 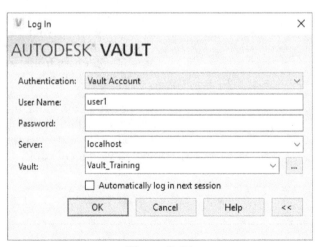 (Autodesk Vault 2021) on the desktop.
   - Select **Autodesk Data Management>Autodesk Vault Professional 2021** from the **Start** menu.
   - Select **Autodesk Vault Professional 2021** in the desktop Apps list.

2. The Log In dialog box opens as shown in Figure 2–24. In the *User Name* field, type **user1**. Verify that *Vault* is set to **Vault_Training** (click [...] (Browse) to select it, as required). Leave the *Password* field blank.

Refer to the Practice Files section of this learning guide to setup the Vault, if not already completed.

Figure 2–24

Selecting this option saves login time.

3. Select **Automatically log in next session** to automatically logged into the vault in subsequent sessions.

4. Click **OK**.

Task 2 - Set a new working folder.

In this task, you will set a new working folder. The vault database has been created with the *AutoCAD Designs A*, *Content Center Files*, *Designs*, and *Documentation* folders created in the Project Explorer ($) root.

1. Select **Project Explorer ($)** and select **File>Set Working Folder**.

2. In the Set Working Folder For '$' To: dialog box, select **C:\Vault Data Management Practice Files\vault_work** and click **Select Folder**.

3. The working folder path can be displayed in the Main table's title bar. To display the path, if not already displayed, select **Tools>Options** and select **Show working folder location**. Click **OK**. Verify that the path is set to *...\vault_work*.

Task 3 - Compare folder structures.

In this task, you will compare the folder structure in the working folder (*...\vault_work*) to the Vault folder structure.

1. To view the working folder, select **Actions>Go To Working Folder**. A File Explorer window opens displaying the working folder contents. Note that there are additional folders shown such as *AutoCAD Designs B* and *AutoCAD Designs C* folders. Close File Explorer.

2. Close File Explorer. View files in the vault.

3. In the Autodesk Vault software, note that there is an *AutoCAD Designs A* folder.

Task 4 - View files in the vault.

In this task, you will use the Preview pane to view and analyze an AutoCAD drawing.

1. In the $\AutoCAD Designs A folder, select **Office.dwg**. In the Preview pane, select the *History* tab, then select the **Show all versions** checkbox to view the history of the file, as shown in Figure 2–25. Note the comments for each version.

History	Uses	Where Used	Change Order	Preview			
Number of versions:		2		(Local = Version #2)			
Number of revisions:		1					☑ Show all versions

Thumbnail	File Name	Version ▽	Created By	Checke...	Comment
▶	Office.dwg	2	Administrator	10/8/20...	Removed elevation
	Office.dwg	1	Administrator	10/8/20...	Initial submission

Figure 2–25

2. In the Preview pane, select the *Preview* tab to view the carousel of versions for this drawing. Select **Version 2** to view Version 2 of the drawing.

3. Select the viewer icons to manipulate and analyze the drawing.

4. In the *Preview* tab, expand the Versions drop-down list and select **Version 1** to display Version 1 of the drawing. Note that Version 2 does not contain the elevation view.

5. Select the *History* tab again and note that the *Comment* column for Version 2 states that the elevation was removed.

Practice 2b

Adding Non-CAD Files to the Vault

Practice Objectives

- Add a non-CAD file to the vault using the **Add Files** command and the drag-and-drop method.
- View a non-CAD file in the vault.

In this practice, you will add non-CAD files to the vault and then display them.

Task 1 - Add non-CAD files to the vault using Add Files.

In this task, you will add a PDF file to the vault using the **Add Files** command.

1. In the Navigation pane, select the $\Documentation folder, right-click, and select **Add Files**.

2. In the C:\Vault Data Management Practice Files\vault_work\ Documentation folder, select the document **Using Autodesk Vault with Single Inventor Project.pdf**, and click **Open**.

3. In the Add Files... dialog box, select **Delete working copies**. In the Enter comments to include... area, type **Initial submission** as shown in Figure 2–26.

Figure 2–26

4. Click **OK**.

Task 2 - Add non-CAD files to the vault using drag and drop.

In this task, you will add a Word file to the vault using drag and drop.

1. In the Navigation pane, select the $\Documentation folder to view its current files.

2. In a File Explorer window, navigate to the *C:\Vault Data Management Practice Files\vault_work\Documentation* folder.

3. Drag **Software Setup.docx** and drop it into the vault *Documentation* folder.

4. In the Add Files... dialog box, select **Delete working copies**. In the *Enter comments to include...* area, type **Initial submission** as shown in Figure 2–27.

Figure 2–27

5. Click **OK**.

Task 3 - View the non-CAD files in the vault.

In this task, you will view the non-CAD files in the vault.

1. In the Main table, select the document **Using Autodesk Vault with Single Inventor Project.pdf**.

2. Switch to the *Preview* tab to display the thumbnail of Version 1. Click the thumbnail to display the PDF in the Preview pane.

3. In the *Preview* tab, click **Open** to open the PDF file in a PDF viewing program outside the Vault.

4. Close the window displaying the PDF file.

5. In the Main table, select **Software Setup.docx**. Click the thumbnail in the *Preview* tab to display the document in the Preview pane.

Chapter Review Questions

1. What is a working folder?

   a. Central repository for data.

   b. A location on the client machine to which design files are downloaded from the vault.

   c. A location in the vault that contains your design files.

   d. All of the above.

2. What are the main areas of the Autodesk Vault interface? (Select all that apply.)

   a. Navigation Pane.

   b. Main Table

   c. Preview Pane

   d. Properties Grid

   e. Toolbars

3. In the Preview pane, the *Where Used* tab lists all of the files used in the selected file.

   a. True

   b. False

4. In the Preview pane, what does the *Uses* tab display when a file is selected from the Project Explorer?

   a. The files that use the selected file.

   b. The files used in the selected file.

   c. The files that reference the selected file.

   d. Only files that are available to use in the selected file.

5. In the Preview pane, the latest version of the selected file displays in the *Preview* tab by default.

   a. True

   b. False

6. Which file format is used for the *Preview* tab to display an image of an Autodesk Inventor file?

    a. DWF

    b. PRT

    c. DWG

    d. PDF

7. How can a non-CAD file be added to the vault for the first time? (Select all that apply.)

    a. Use the **Check In** command.

    b. Drag and drop from File Explorer.

    c. Use the **Add Files** command.

    d. Use the **New Folder** command.

Command Summary

Button	Command	Location
	Add Files	• Standard toolbar
	Attachments	• Standard toolbar
	Auto Preview	• Advanced toolbar
	Autodesk App Store Manager	• Standard toolbar
Check In...	**Check In**	• Standard toolbar
	Copy Design	• Standard toolbar
	Delete	• Standard toolbar
	Expand the query builder	• Main Table pane
Find...	**Find**	• Standard toolbar
	Fit to Window	• Preview pane
	Get	• Standard toolbar
	Group By Box	• Advanced toolbar
Layout ▾	**Layout**	• Advanced toolbar
	Measure Length	• Preview pane
	Move Backward	• Advanced toolbar
	Move Forward	• Advanced toolbar
New ▾	**New Folder** or **New Library Folder**	• Standard toolbar
	Orbit	• Preview pane
	Pan the Canvas	• Preview pane
	Preview pane	• Advanced toolbar
	Print Direct	• Standard toolbar
	Print Preview	• Standard toolbar

	Refresh	• **Standard toolbar**
	Undo Check Out	• **Standard toolbar**
	Up One Level	• **Advanced toolbar**
	Zoom Area	• **Preview pane**
	Zoom In/Out	• **Preview pane**

Orientation to the AutoCAD Vault Integration Add-in

The AutoCAD Vault Add-in provides direct access to the Autodesk® Vault software in the AutoCAD interface. This integration enables you to perform many of the tasks available using the Autodesk Vault software. In this chapter, you learn about the AutoCAD Vault Add-in interface, which includes using the External References palette (Xref Manager) for performing vault activities. You also learn how to add AutoCAD files to the vault for the first time.

Learning Objectives in This Chapter

- Log in to the Autodesk Vault software from the AutoCAD software.
- Differentiate between using **Open** in the Quick Access Toolbar and **Open** in the *Vault* tab in the Access panel.
- Check the status of AutoCAD files located in the vault using the External References palette in the AutoCAD software.
- Upload AutoCAD files to the vault using the **Check In** and **Check In Folder** commands.

3.1 Log In to Vault from AutoCAD

You can log in to the Autodesk Vault software from the AutoCAD interface.

How To: Launch AutoCAD and Log In to the Vault

1. Launch the AutoCAD software.
2. In the *Vault* tab>Access panel, click **Log In** as shown in Figure 3–1.

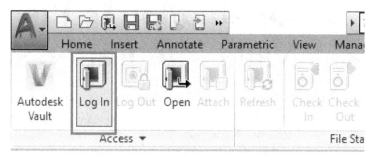

Figure 3–1

*After you have logged in for the first time, the server and vault names are stored so that the same information displays each time you log in to the vault. Select **Automatically log in next session** to log in automatically and bypass the Log In window.*

3. Enter your user name and password as shown in Figure 3–2.

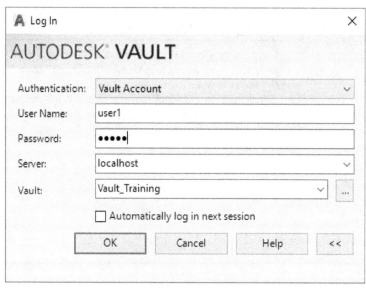

Figure 3–2

4. Click **OK**.

3.2 Retrieve AutoCAD Files from the Vault

Open from Vault

In the AutoCAD software, if you click (Open) in the Quick Access Toolbar rather than (Open) in the *Vault* tab>Access panel, you are prompted to select a file from the local workspace. The workspace is a local folder that is mapped to the corresponding folder in the vault. The workspace can be a single folder, or can include an hierarchy of subfolders to help organize the design. The recommended best practice is to use

(Open) in the *Vault* tab>Access panel to open the file from the vault instead of from the local working folder. This ensures that you are always working with the latest version of the project.

If you click (Open) without logging in, you are prompted to log in.

(Open) in the *Vault* tab>Access panel in the integrated user interface is available after you log in to the vault, as shown in Figure 3–3.

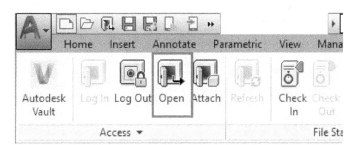

Figure 3–3

How To: Open a File from the Vault

1. In the AutoCAD software, in the *Vault* tab>Access panel, click
   (Open). The Select File dialog box opens, as shown in Figure 3–4.

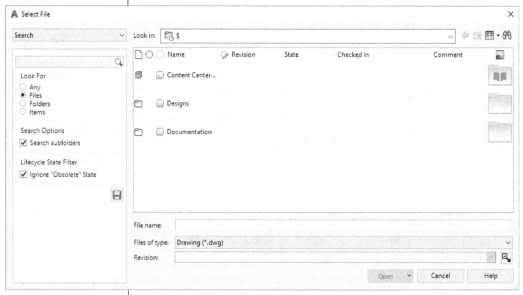

Figure 3–4

You can use *(Advanced Search) to access the Find dialog box.*

You can use to *save your search, once executed, to **My Saved Searches** for reuse purposes.*

2. You can navigate the folder structure to select the required file, or you can search using the field shown in Figure 3–5.

3. You can also locate a file using **My Saved Searches** or **My Shortcuts**, as shown in Figure 3–6.

Figure 3–5

Figure 3–6

4. When you click on a file to select it, the latest revision of that file in the vault is selected by default and **Latest** displays in the *Revision* field. If a different revision is required, select one from the Revision drop-down list, as shown in Figure 3–7.

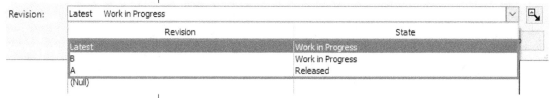

Figure 3–7

5. Select 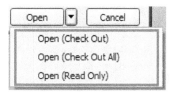 next to **Open** and select one of the open methods, as shown in Figure 3–8.

Figure 3–8

- **Open (Check Out):** Check out and open the file.
- **Open (Check Out All):** Check out and open the selected file and all of its children.
- **Open (Read Only):** Open the file without checking it out.

6. If you do not select one of the methods shown in Figure 3–8, you can click **Open** to retrieve the file from the vault into the AutoCAD software. You are prompted to check out the file.

7. Click **No** to open the file as read-only or click **Yes** and then **OK** to check the file out of the vault.

Attach from Vault

To add an image or drawing from the vault to an AutoCAD drawing, click 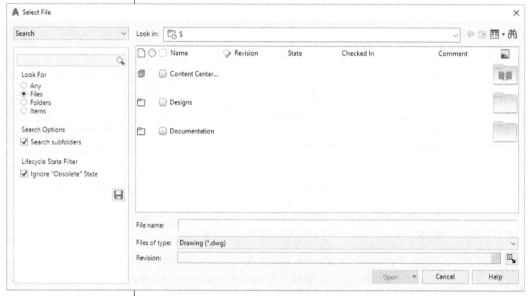 (Attach) in the *Vault* tab>Access panel. The Select File dialog box opens.

The options in this dialog box are the same as the ones displayed when **Open From Vault** is selected, as shown in Figure 3–9.

Figure 3–9

3.3 Using the External References (XREF) Palette

The AutoCAD Vault Add-in adds vaulting functionality to the External References palette (also known as the Xref Manager). In addition to performing standard XREF operations such as managing relationships between a host file and its XREFs, the External References palette enables you to perform all vaulting tasks when logged into the vault, including viewing the status of AutoCAD files within the vault.

When AutoCAD Vault is installed, the External References palette becomes a dockable Enhanced Standard Window (ESW) that supports both drawing XREFs and image files in the same window.

Accessing the Xref Manager

How To: Access the External References Palette (Xref Manager):

1. Click 🗔 (External References Palette) in the *View* tab>Palettes panel, as shown in Figure 3–10.

Figure 3–10

2. The External References palette displays as shown in Figure 3–11.

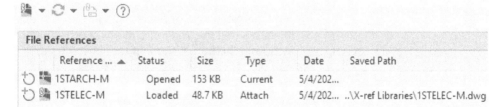

Figure 3–11

3. Once it displays, you can choose to dock the palette to the left- or right-hand side of the window and set to auto-hide for ease of use. To do this, right-click on the EXTERNAL REFERENCES vertical column and select **Allow Docking**, **Anchor Left** (or **Anchor Right**) and **Auto-hide**, as shown in Figure 3–12.

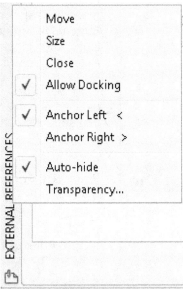

Figure 3–12

If the column containing the vault status icon is hidden, stretch the right-hand side of the column until the icon displays.

In the External References palette, to the left-hand side of each reference name, is the standard AutoCAD document icon. If you are logged into the vault, another column appears on the left-hand side of the AutoCAD document icon, displaying the vault status icon. The vault status icons are as follows:

- A white circle with a plus sign indicates that the files are not yet in the vault.

- A plain white circle or a white circle with a checkmark indicates that the version of file you are working with is in sync with the Latest Version that is in the vault.

Viewing the File Status Using the External References Palette

How To: View the Vault Status in the External References Palette

1. Hover the cursor over the vault status icon in the palette to view the vault status tool tip, as shown in Figure 3–13. This tooltip provides information on the action to be performed on the file.

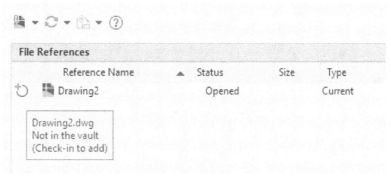

Figure 3–13

2. Select a file and right-click to see the commands. The commands available depend on how the file was opened and if it is an XREF or a host file. For example, if you checked out the file when opening it, **Check In** is available but not **Check Out**.

XREF Operations

The list of XREF operations available for the host and XREF files in the External References palette is described in the following table.

Option	File Type	Description
Open	XREF only	Opens the selected XREF to view it.
Attach	XREF only	Attaches another instance of the xref to the drawing.
Unload	XREF only	Unloads the selected XREFs. The reference can be loaded at a later time.
Reload	Host and XREF	Opens a copy of a file's latest checked in version to your computer and loads it into memory. **Note:** When you currently have a file checked out to you and it is newer than the one in the vault, the reload command reloads from the working folder, and not from the vault.
Detach	XREF only	Detaches one or more XREFs from your drawing, erasing all instances of a specified XREF.
Bind	XREF only	Converts a selected XREF into a block, making it part of your drawing permanently.
Check In	Host and XREF	Uploads a file from the working folder to the vault.
Check Out	Host and XREF	Copies a file from the vault to the client's working folder to perform a change operation.
Undo Check Out	Host and XREF	Checks the selected file(s) back in, unmodified.

Vault Status Icons

- A white circle with a plus sign ( ) indicates that the files are not in the vault.

- If a filename displays in **bold font**, it means that the file is checked out to you. An asterisk beside the filename indicates that you have changes in memory that have not been saved, and it requires a save before it can be added to the vault.

- A white circle containing a checkmark ( ) or nothing ( ) indicates that the version of file you are working with is the same as the one in the vault. This is also known as the *Latest Version* and is typically preferred for use.

3.4 Check In AutoCAD Files to Vault

Since the Autodesk Vault software does not track and maintain relationships between AutoCAD files, it is recommended that you use the Vault Add-in for AutoCAD to add AutoCAD files to the Vault (i.e., use the External References palette or the *Vault* tab options instead of the Autodesk Vault client).

The **Check In** and **Check In Folder** operations can be used to add your files to the vault for the first time. Autodesk .DWF files are created and attached automatically for files that have changed or for files that do not already have .DWF files published. Vault hides the published .DWF files from the Main Table.

Only one file can be checked in at a time unless it is a host file that references other files. When a host file is added to the vault, all dependent files are added automatically, retaining the saved paths to all the files it references.

A CAD file becomes the master when it is added or checked into the vault. Use the **Get Revision** operation to update the local working folder with the latest version (leading version of the leading revision) of the selected files. Use **Check Out** when you want to modify the files. These operations copy the requested files to your local working folder again and ensure that you are working with the latest versions.

> ### Best Practice: Temporarily Store Files in the Local Working Folder
>
> As a recommended best practice, the working folder should be considered a temporary folder in which to store files until they are checked back into the vault. Once checked back into the vault, the temporary files should be deleted.

Check In

Only DWG and image files can be checked into the vault in AutoCAD. To check other file types into the vault, use the Autodesk Vault client interface.

How To: Check In Files to the Vault

1. Log in to the Vault and open an AutoCAD drawing from a local folder.
2. Use one of the following methods to access the **Check In** command:
   - Select **Check In** in the *Vault* tab>Access panel.
   - In the External References palette, select the file, right-click, and click **Check In**.
3. The Select Vault Location dialog box opens as shown in Figure 3–14.

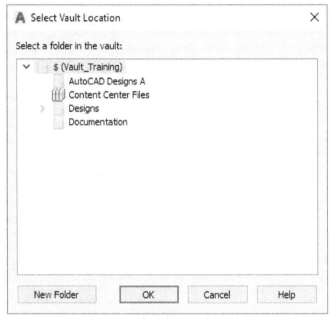

Figure 3–14

4. Select the Vault Location by selecting the existing vault folder. You can also select **New Folder** to create a new vault folder.
5. Select **OK** in the Select Vault Location dialog box.
6. If you have not saved the files, you will be prompted to do so. Select **Yes** to save.
7. The Check In dialog opens, as shown in Figure 3–15.

Figure 3–15

The vault creates any folders required to support the structure displayed in the dialog box.

8. Select **Keep files checked out** to check the files into the vault and then check them out again so that you can keep working with them.

9. Select **Close files and delete working copies** to close the files after they have been checked in and delete them from the local working folder.

10. Click **Settings** to set the .DWF attachment settings. To create the visualization files, select either the **Create during check-in** option or the **Send to Job Server** option. The **Apply to all files** option can also be selected with preferences regarding Model Tab and Layout Tabs, as shown in Figure 3–16.

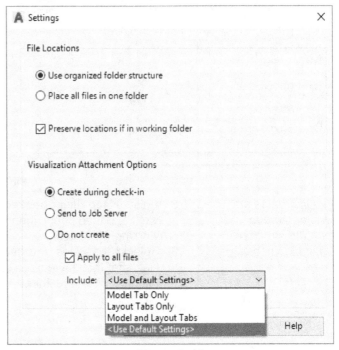

Figure 3–16

11. Click **OK**.
12. In the *Enter comments to include...* area, enter comments as required.
13. Click **OK**.

Check In Folder

The **Check In Folder** operation enables you to add an entire folder and its recursive contents to the vault in a single operation.

How To: Check In a Folder of Files

1. In the Application Menu, expand Vault Server and select
   Check In Folder as shown in Figure 3–17.

Figure 3–17

2. In the Check In Folder dialog, select the folder to check in and the target vault location, if required, as shown in Figure 3–18.

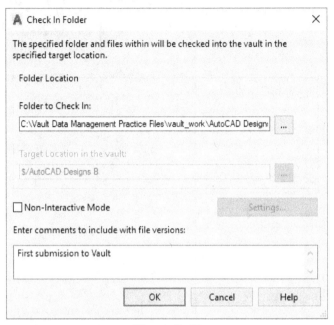

Figure 3–18

3. In the *Enter comments to include...* area, enter comments as required.
4. Click **OK**.
5. A Check In Details dialog will open showing the results of the check in, as shown in Figure 3–19.

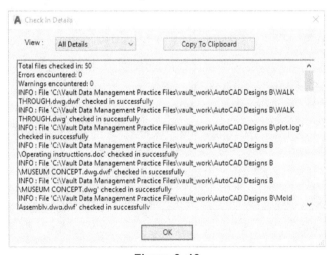

Figure 3–19

6. Click **OK**.

Add Library Files

Library files can also be added to the vault using the **Check In** and **Check In Folder** operations.

Categories

Categories enable you to group objects and assign a defined set of behaviors and rules to objects. For example, a category can automatically assign user-defined properties to objects in the Vault, automatically assign lifecycle definitions, or automatically set revision values to files.

How To: Change a Category

1. Select an object and then select **Change Category** from the toolbar or from the **Actions** menu.

You can also change the category of a file from within AutoCAD from the Vault tab>Control panel or from the External References palette shortcut menu.

2. Select a new category from the drop-down list, as shown in Figure 3–20.

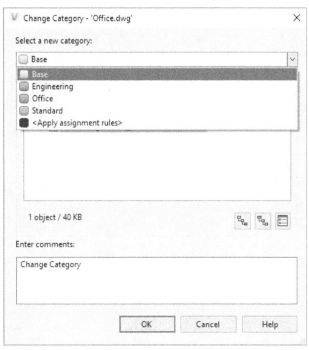

Figure 3–20

3. Click **OK**.

Practice 3a

Orientation to the AutoCAD Add-in Interface

Practice Objectives

- Log in to the Autodesk Vault software from within AutoCAD.
- Open a drawing and display the External References palette.
- Check In a drawing to the vault.
- Use the External References palette to view vault status.

In this practice, you are oriented to the Vault AutoCAD Add-in interface. You first launch AutoCAD and log in to the vault. Using the External References palette with its vault capabilities you view the vault status of AutoCAD drawing files.

Task 1 - Launch AutoCAD and log in to the vault.

1. Launch the AutoCAD software. Create a new drawing and select a template so that the *Vault* tab becomes active.

2. In the *Vault* tab>Access panel, click **Login**.

3. Type **user1** as the user name. Do not enter a password, as shown in Figure 3–21.

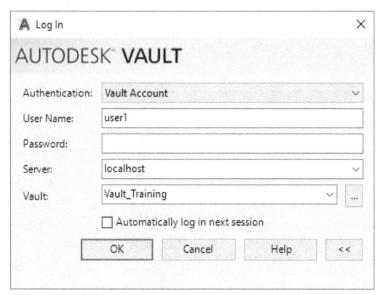

Figure 3–21

4. Click **OK**.

Task 2 - Open an AutoCAD drawing.

In this task, even though you are now logged in to the vault, you open an AutoCAD drawing from your local folders using the Open command.

1. Select **Open** from the applications menu.

2. Select **TANK.dwg** from the ...\vault_work\AutoCAD Designs B directory, as shown in Figure 3–22.

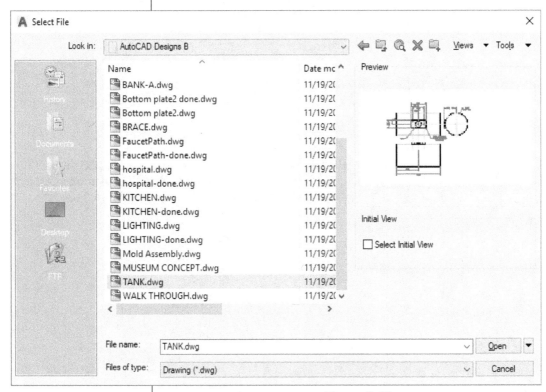

Figure 3–22

3. Select **Open** to display the drawing in the AutoCAD software.

Task 3 - Display the External References palette.

In this task, you display the External References palette (also known as the Xref Manager), which is used for vault activities in addition to its standard XREF capabilities. For ease of use, you dock the External References palette and set it to auto-hide.

1. Open the External References palette by clicking
   ▢ (External References Palette) in the *View* tab>Palettes
   pane, as shown in Figure 3–23.

Figure 3–23

2. Right-click on the EXTERNAL REFERENCES vertical
   column and ensure that **Allow Docking**, **Anchor Left** and
   Auto-hide are selected, as shown in Figure 3–24.

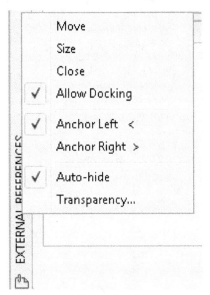

Figure 3–24

Task 4 - View the vault status using the External References palette.

In this task, you become familiar with using the External References palette to view the vault status of AutoCAD files.

1. In the External References palette (Xref Manager), there is a white circle with a plus sign (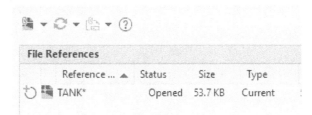) next to the reference name, as shown in Figure 3–25.

Figure 3–25

2. Move your cursor over the circle with the plus sign icon to see a tool tip indicating that the file is not in the vault and a recommendation to use **Check In**.

Task 5 - Check in the drawing to the vault.

1. Select TANK in the External References palette, right-click, and click **Check In** in the pop-up menu, as shown in Figure 3–26.

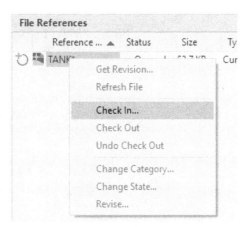

Figure 3–26

2. Click **Yes** to save the file.

3. The file was opened from the working folder structure, therefore in the Check In dialog box, *$/AutoCAD Designs B* is automatically selected as the vault folder location, as shown in Figure 3–27.

Figure 3–27

4. Type **Initial submission to vault** in the comments area.

5. Click **OK** to proceed with the check in operation.

Task 6 - View the vault status in the External References palette.

1. In the External References palette, the vault status icon has changed to just a white circle, indicating that the file is now in the vault and that you are working with the latest version, as shown in Figure 3–28.

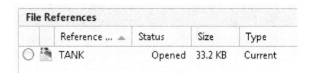

Figure 3–28

2. Close the drawing.

Practice 3b

Adding a Folder of Files to the Vault

Practice Objectives

- Open a drawing with an XREF and open the External References palette.
- Add folders of AutoCAD files to the vault.
- View file relationships within Autodesk Vault.

In this practice, you add entire folders of files to the vault using the **Check In Folder** command. Some of these files are host files with XREFs that also need to be added and their relationships maintained.

Task 1 - Open a drawing with an XREF and open the External References palette.

In this task, you open a drawing containing an XREF and display the External References palette to show the XREF information and its vault status.

1. Open **1STARCH-M.dwg** from **...vault_work\AutoCAD Designs B**, as shown in Figure 3–29.

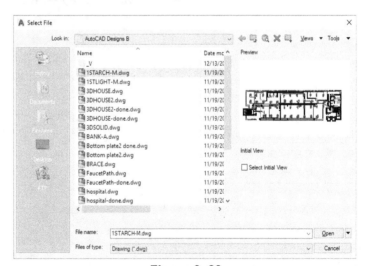

Figure 3–29

2. Select **Open** to display the drawing in AutoCAD.

3. Open the External References palette. The white circles with plus signs beside the reference names indicate that they are not in the vault, as shown in Figure 3–30.

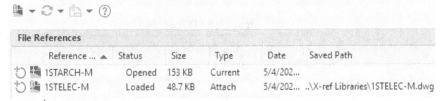

Reference ... ▲	Status	Size	Type	Date	Saved Path
1STARCH-M	Opened	153 KB	Current	5/4/202...	
1STELEC-M	Loaded	48.7 KB	Attach	5/4/202...	..\X-ref Libraries\1STELEC-M.dwg

Figure 3–30

- **1STELEC-M** is an XREF, as indicated by the Type column displaying "Attach" and the Status column displaying "Loaded". The XREF resides in the folder *...vault_work\X-ref Libraries*, which can be seen in the saved path location for **1STELEC-M**.

Task 2 - Check in the first folder of AutoCAD files into the vault.

In this task, you check into the vault the entire folder of AutoCAD files where **1STARCH-M.dwg** resides.

1. Select **Vault Server>Check In Folder** from the application menu, as shown in Figure 3–31.

Figure 3–31

2. Select ...\vault_work\AutoCAD Designs B as the folder to check in and type **First submission to Vault** in the comments area. The target vault location is specified as *$/AutoCAD Designs B*, as shown in Figure 3–32.

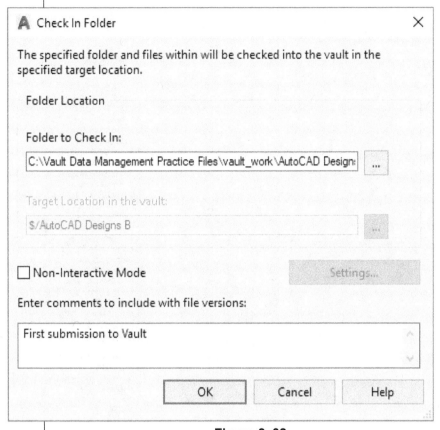

Figure 3–32

3. Select **OK**.

4. The Check in Folder dialog box appears showing all files to be added to the vault, including the folder structure that is created, as shown in Figure 3–33. The 1**STELEC-M.dwg** is shown under the *X-ref Libraries* folder.

Figure 3–33

5. Select **Settings**. Select the options as shown in Figure 3–34.

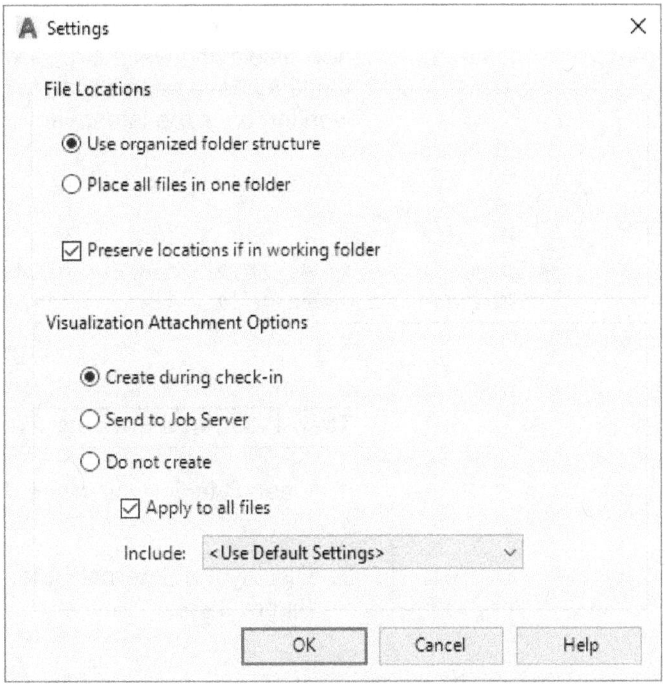

Figure 3–34

6. Select **OK** in the Settings dialog box. You can also move the cursor over the ⬛ icon in the Check In Folder dialog box to see that the DWF Create visualization attachment option is toggled On.

7. Select **OK** to check the files in to the vault.

8. Select **OK** after confirming results in the Check In Details dialog box.

Task 3 - View vault status of the drawing and XREF.

Open the External References palette. The vault status icons are now displaying white circles without the plus signs, indicating that they have been added to the vault, and that the copy you are working on is the latest version, as shown in Figure 3–35.

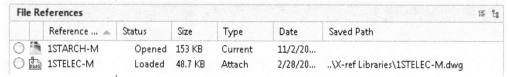

		Reference ... ▲	Status	Size	Type	Date	Saved Path
○		1STARCH-M	Opened	153 KB	Current	11/2/20...	
○		1STELEC-M	Loaded	48.7 KB	Attach	2/28/20...	..\X-ref Libraries\1STELEC-M.dwg

Figure 3–35

Task 4 - Open a drawing from a second folder.

1. Open **Site Survey-done.dwg** from ...\vault_work\AutoCAD Designs C.

2. Display the External References palette as shown in Figure 3–36.

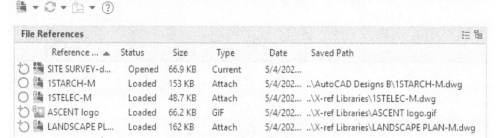

		Reference ... ▲	Status	Size	Type	Date	Saved Path
		SITE SURVEY-d...	Opened	66.9 KB	Current	5/4/202...	
○		1STARCH-M	Loaded	153 KB	Attach	5/4/202...	..\AutoCAD Designs B\1STARCH-M.dwg
○		1STELEC-M	Loaded	48.7 KB	Attach	5/4/202...	..\X-ref Libraries\1STELEC-M.dwg
		ASCENT logo	Loaded	66.2 KB	GIF	5/4/202...	..\X-ref Libraries\ASCENT logo.gif
		LANDSCAPE PL...	Loaded	162 KB	Attach	5/4/202...	..\X-ref Libraries\LANDSCAPE PLAN-M.dwg

Figure 3–36

3. The **Site Survey-done.dwg** references the **1STELEC-M xref** and the **1STARCH-M.dwg**, which are indicated as already being added to the vault.

Task 5 - Check in the second folder of AutoCAD files into the vault.

In this task, you check in another folder of AutoCAD files into the vault.

1. Select **Vault Server>Check In Folder** from the application menu.

2. Select ...\vault_work\AutoCAD Designs C as the folder to check in and type **First submission to Vault** in the comments area. The vault target location is automatically selected as $/AutoCAD Designs C.

3. Select **OK**.

4. The Check in Folder dialog box appears showing all files to be added to the vault, including the folder structure that is used and/or created, as shown in Figure 3–37.

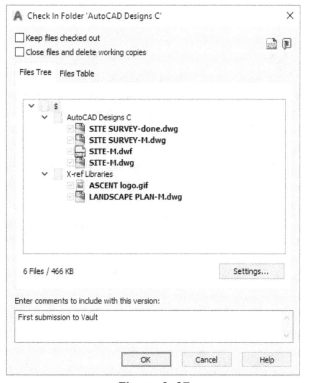

Figure 3–37

5. Select **OK** to add the files to the vault.

6. Select **OK** after confirming the results in the Check In Details dialog box.

Task 6 - Verify files in the vault.

In this task, you verify that the files in the folder have been added to the vault and the relationships have been maintained.

1. If Autodesk Vault was closed, launch it again by clicking Autodesk Vault in the *Vault* tab>Access panel, as shown in Figure 3–38.

Figure 3–38

2. Log in as **user1** with no password.

3. Select 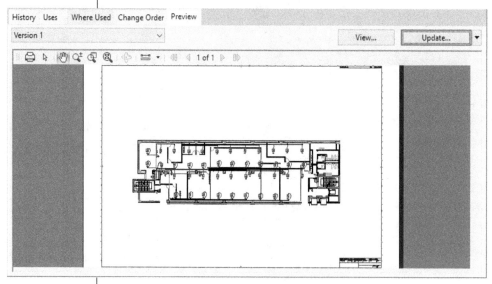 (Refresh) to update the vault folders.

4. In the Navigation pane, the *AutoCAD Designs B*, *AutoCAD Designs C* and *X-ref Libraries* folders were created under *$* during the **Check In Folder** operations.

5. Select *$/AutoCAD Designs B*.

6. Select the *History* tab for several of the files to see that they are all Version 1 since they were all just added to the Vault for the first time.

7. Select **1STARCH-M.dwg**. Select the *Preview* tab in the Preview pane. Select the Version 1 thumbnail. The drawing is displayed, as shown in Figure 3–39, because a .DWF was created during the process of adding the files.

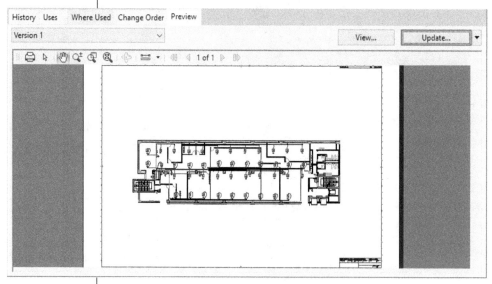

Figure 3–39

8. Select the *Where Used* tab in the Preview pane. Relationships have been maintained between the files, as shown in Figure 3–40.

Figure 3–40

9. Select the *Uses* tab in the Preview pane. **1STELEC-M.dwg** is a child of **1STARCH-M.dwg** and their relationship was maintained upon check in, as shown in Figure 3–41.

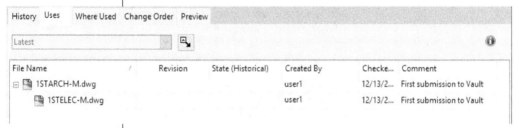

Figure 3–41

10. Select *$/AutoCAD Designs C* in the Navigation pane and select **SITE SURVEY-done.dwg** in the Main Table.

11. Select the *Uses* tab in the Preview pane. **1STARCH-M.dwg** and **1STELEC.M.dwg** are children of **SITE SURVEY-done.dwg** and other children are being referenced from the *$/X-ref Libraries* folder with their relationships intact after the two **Check In Folder** operations, as shown in Figure 3–42.

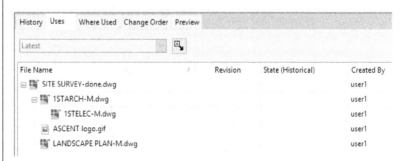

Figure 3–42

Practice 3c

Using Open from the Vault and Attach from the Vault

Practice Objectives

- Use Open from the vault to open an AutoCAD drawing from the vault.
- Use Attach from the vault to attach a reference file from the vault to an AutoCAD drawing.

In this practice, you use Open from the vault to open an AutoCAD design from the vault. As well, you then use Attach from the vault to attach an XREF from the vault to an AutoCAD drawing.

Task 1 - Open an AutoCAD drawing from the vault.

In this task, you open **Mold Assembly.dwg** using the **Open from Vault** command.

1. In AutoCAD, from the *Vault* tab>Access panel, click

    (Open from the vault). It opens directly into the vault folder structure.

2. Browse to the *$/AutoCAD Designs B* vault folder and then select the **Mold Assembly.dwg**, as shown in Figure 3–43.

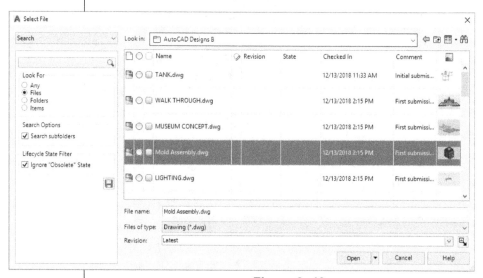

Figure 3–43

3. Select **Open**.

4. A warning message appears indicating that the file has not been checked out and prompts whether you want to check it out now, as shown in Figure 3–44.

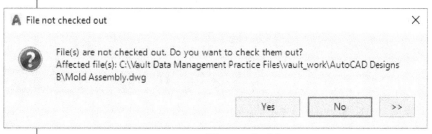

Figure 3–44

5. Select **Yes** to check out the drawing.

6. Open the External References palette. The vault status icon displays a white circle with a check mark indicating that the file is checked out to you and is the latest version, as shown in Figure 3–45.

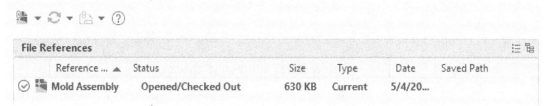

Figure 3–45

Task 2 - Use Attach from the vault.

You could also access **Attach from Vault** *from the External References palette.*

1. In AutoCAD, from the *Vault* tab>Access panel, click

     (Attach from the vault).

2. In the Select File dialog box, select Files of type to **All image files** then browse to *$/X-ref Libraries* and select **ASCENT logo.gif**, as shown in Figure 3–46.

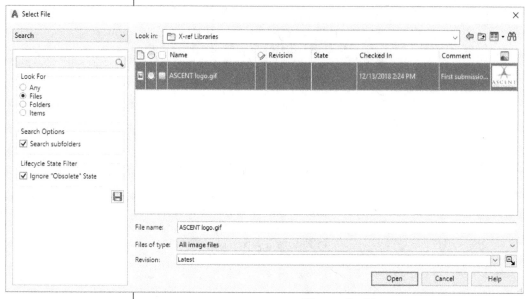

Figure 3–46

3. Select **Open** and **Yes** to check out.

4. To place the XREF, select the **Specify on-screen** option in the Attach Image dialog box as shown in Figure 3–47.

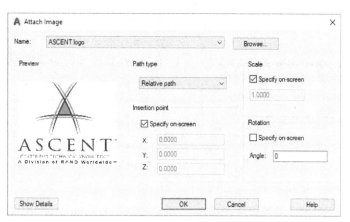

Figure 3–47

5. Click **OK**.

6. Place the logo XREF anywhere on the assembly.

7. Click 🖫 to save the change to the drawing.

8. Open the External References palette. The vault status displays as shown in Figure 3–48.

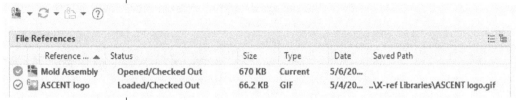

Figure 3–48

9. In the External References palette, select **Mold Assembly**, right-click, and click **Check In**.

10. Type **ASCENT logo added** in the comments area and click **OK**, as shown in Figure 3–49. Note that the logo is checked in as well.

Figure 3–49

11. Close **Mold Assembly**.

12. In Autodesk Vault, select **Mold Assembly.dwg** from the *$/AutoCAD Designs B* vault folder.

13. In the *Preview* tab, display both Version 1 and Version 2 of the design using the Version drop-down list, as shown in Figure 3–50.

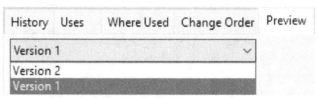

Figure 3–50

14. Notice that the logo displays in Version 2.

15. Close all drawings.

Chapter Review Questions

1. When you use **Open** from the *Vault* tab in AutoCAD, what are the three options to open your file that are located in the **Open** drop-down list? (Select all that apply)

   a. Open (Check Out All)

   b. Open Read-Only

   c. Open (Check Out)

   d. Open (Check In)

2. The Xref Manager is another name for the External References palette.

   a. True

   b. False

3. In the External References palette, what does it mean when a file name appears with a white circle and plus sign beside it?

   a. The files are not yet in the vault.

   b. You are not working on the Latest Version.

   c. The file is not available for Check Out.

   d. All of the above.

4. What does the vault status icon look like when the version you are making changes to is the same as the one in the vault? (Select all that apply.)

   a. Question mark

   b. White circle with plus sign

   c. White circle with checkmark

   d. White circle

5. What command is used to associate a library or reference file within Vault to a design file?

   a. Open

   b. Attach from Vault

   c. Open from Vault

   d. Check Out

6. The Check In Folder command can be used to load your legacy data into the vault.

   a. True

   b. False

Chapter

4

Searching the Vault

The Autodesk® Vault software provides a variety of search methods to locate files in the database. You can use a basic text string search or an advanced search on one or more file properties. Vaults can also be configured by the Administrator to perform a full content search of known file formats. Specialized searches enable you to easily locate specific objects in a large database.

Learning Objectives in This Chapter

- Differentiate between the search methods available in Autodesk Vault.
- Locate files using each search method.
- Create a saved search, edit a saved search, and run a saved search.
- Manage saved searches using the **Rename**, **Copy**, and **Delete** commands.
- Create a search report.

4.1 Overview of Search Methods

Locating a file quickly and easily becomes important when design projects and databases contain a large number of files. Since Vault stores file properties and indexes them in the database, they can quickly be queried to locate a particular file.

Four main search operations enable you to locate files in the database: **Browse Folders**, **Quick Search**, **Basic Find**, and **Advanced Find**.

Use this table to compare search methods and decide which method best suits your needs.

Search Tool	Description
Browse Folders	Enables you to navigate the folder structure in the Navigation pane to find and view design folders and files. Click ⊞ (Expand) to expand the folder structure and ⊟ (Collapse) to collapse it (similar to File Explorer). ⊟ Project Explorer ($) ⊞ Content Center Files ⊟ Designs ⊞ Arm System ⊞ Hub Shaft ⊞ Mold Assembly ⊞ Piston ⊞ Top Plate ⊞ Vise ⊞ Yoke ⊞ Documentation ⊞ My Search Folders
Quick Search	The Quick Search is located in the Main table title bar. Quick Search enables you to search on all of the file properties in the folders based on a specified text string. You can also click ⊗ (Expand the query builder) to set specific property search criteria and ▾ (Show search options menu) to access additional search options.

Basic Find	The Basic Find is located in the Find dialog box and enables you to search by entering a specified text string. The search locates any file or object in the vault that contains the search string in any of the file properties. 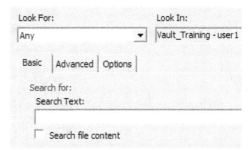
Advanced Find	The Advanced Find is located in the Find dialog box and enables you to create advanced searches by specifying file property criteria. The search locates the files and objects that match that criteria. 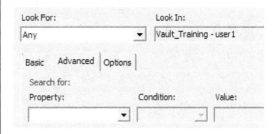

Searches defined using Quick Search or the Find dialog box (**Basic** or **Advanced**) can be saved to be used again. For quick access, any saved search can be added to *My Search Folders* in the Navigation pane. You can also select the saved search from the Select File dialog boxes in the AutoCAD software.

Wildcard and Boolean Operators

Wildcards and Boolean operators can be used in **Basic** and **Advanced Find** operations.

Wildcard Operators

Wildcard	Description
*	Represents any characters.
?	Represents a single character.

Boolean Operators (case insensitive)

Operator	Description
and	Search results return anything containing both words.
or	Search results return anything containing either word.
not	The search results exclude anything containing the specified word.
" "	The search results return everything containing the exact phrase in the quotes.

4.2 Browsing Folder Structure

In the Autodesk Vault software, you can browse the created folder structure to search for files. This is useful when you know the folder or design name and want to view its associated files.

To browse, click ⊞ (Expand) to display the expanded folder structure. When the design folder is found and selected, its associated files display in the Main pane on the right side. An example of a selected design file is shown in Figure 4–1.

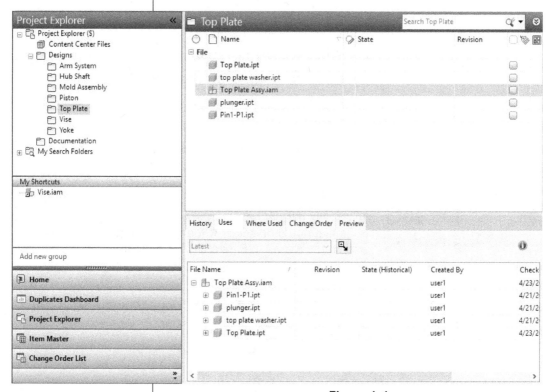

Figure 4–1

4.3 Quick Search

The **Quick Search** performs a search on all of the file properties in the folders based on the specified text string. **Quick Search** is located in the Main table's title bar, as shown in Figure 4–2.

Figure 4–2

How To: Perform a Quick Search

1. In the *Search* field, enter a text string.

2. Click 🔍 (Search) or press <Enter>. The search results display.

3. Click ✕ (Clear or cancel search) to return to the contents of the main table.

Recent Searches

To access a list of recent searches, click ▾ (Show search options menu) and select **Recent Searches**. Select a recent search (as shown in Figure 4–3) to execute the search.

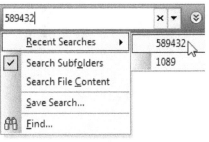

Figure 4–3

Query Builder

To specify additional criteria for your search, click 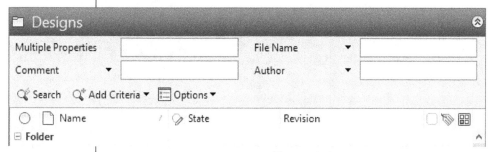 (Expand the query builder) in the title bar to expand the Query Builder, as shown in Figure 4–4.

Figure 4–4

How To: Add Search Criteria Using Query Builder

1. Click ⊗ to expand the Query Builder.
2. In the *Multiple Properties* field, enter the value that you want to search for in the properties.
3. If required, enter values in the *File Name, Comment,* and *Author* fields.

The Query Builder properties selected are kept from session to session.

4. To add a search for a specific property, click **Add Criteria** and select the property. For example, the **Part Number** property is selected (as shown in Figure 4–5) and added as a property to search (as shown in Figure 4–6).

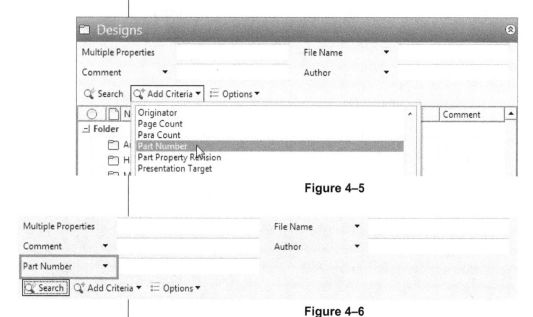

Figure 4–5

Figure 4–6

5. You can also change an existing property to another property or delete a property by clicking the down arrow next to the property name, as shown in Figure 4–7.

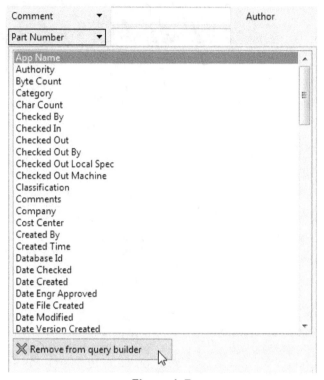

Figure 4–7

6. Click **Search** to execute the search and display the search results.

4.4 Basic Find

The **Basic Find** performs a search on all file properties in the folders based on the specified text string. You can access the **Basic Find** functionality in the *Basic* tab in the Find dialog box. Click **Find...** in the Standard toolbar to open the Find dialog box. You can also open the Find dialog box by selecting **Tools>Find** or pressing <Ctrl>+<F>. The Find dialog box opens as shown in Figure 4–8.

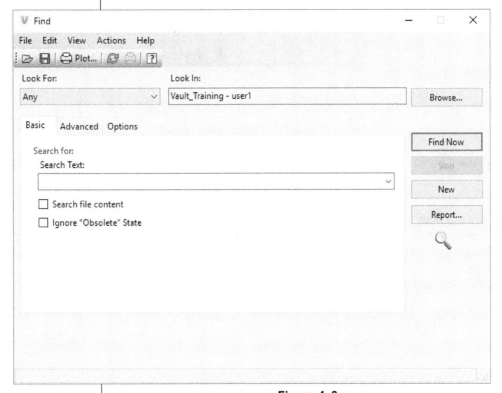

Figure 4–8

Specify which folders to search by clicking **Browse...** next to *Look In*. Select **Search file content** to search the contents of files. The Content Indexing Service must be enabled in the Autodesk Vault Manager to perform a full content search.

How To: Perform a Basic Find

1. In the Find dialog box, select the *Basic* tab.
2. For *Look In*, browse to the vault folder that you want to search. By default, the entire vault is searched. To refine the search, click **Browse...** and select the folders to be searched. To search the contents of the files, select **Search file content**.

The Search Text drop-down list stores the 10 most recent searches.

3. Enter the required keywords, including any wildcards or boolean operators to help define the search.
4. Select the *Options* tab to confirm or clear the optional settings shown in Figure 4–9.

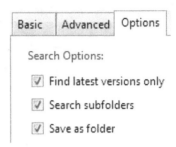

Figure 4–9

5. Press <Enter> or click **Find Now** to execute the search.
6. The search results display at the bottom of the Find dialog box, in which you can sort or customize the columns. You can perform actions on the resulting files by right-clicking and selecting an option.

*You can also expand **Actions** and select an option to modify the files.*

7. Click **New** if you want to define a new search.

4.5 Advanced Find

An **Advanced Find** provides greater flexibility over the search criteria. In the *Advanced* tab in the Find dialog box, you can define more in-depth search criteria using *Property*, *Condition*, and *Value*, as shown in Figure 4–10.

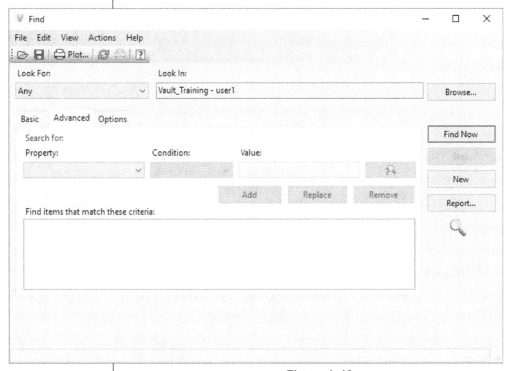

Figure 4–10

How To: Perform an Advanced Find

1. In the Find dialog box, select the *Advanced* tab.
2. For *Look In*, browse to the vault folder that you want to search. By default, the entire vault is searched. Click **Browse...** to refine the search by selecting specific folders.
3. Expand the Property drop-down list and select an option.

Custom properties are also available for searching.

4. Expand the Condition drop-down list and select an option. The conditions for a text field are shown in Figure 4–11.

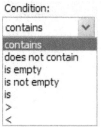

Condition:

contains
- contains
- does not contain
- is empty
- is not empty
- is
- >
- <

Figure 4–11

5. The options available in the drop-down list depend on the type of Property selected. For example, the Conditions for a date field include: **is, before, after, on or before, on or after, Yesterday, Today, Tomorrow, Last # Days, Next # Days, Last Week, This Week**, and **Next Week**, while those for a numeric field include: **is, <=, <, >=, >**, and **is not**.

6. In the *Value* field, enter the value for the condition.

7. Click **Add** to add the properties to the list of criteria.

8. Repeat Steps 3 to 6 to add more properties to refine the search results.

9. If you need to remove any of the search criteria, select them in the *Find items that match these criteria* field and click **Remove**.

10. Select the *Options* tab to confirm or clear the optional settings shown in Figure 4–12.

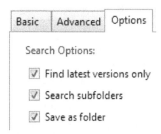

Basic	Advanced	Options

Search Options:

☑ Find latest versions only

☑ Search subfolders

☑ Save as folder

Figure 4–12

11. When the search criteria and settings have been defined, click **Find Now** to execute the search.

12. The search results display at the bottom of the dialog box. You can sort or customize the columns, and perform actions on the files by right-clicking and selecting an option.

13. Click **New** to define a new search.

You can also expand **Actions** *and select an option to modify the files.*

4.6 Saving Searches

Once you have defined a search, you can save the search criteria so that you can perform the same search again. In addition to defining and saving searches, the Find dialog box enables you to open and manage saved searches.

How To: Save a Search for Reuse

You can also click 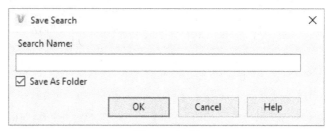 *(Save Current Search) in the Find toolbar.*

1. In the Find dialog box, select **File>Save Search** when your search results display.
2. For *Search Name*, type a name for the saved search in the Save Search dialog box, as shown in Figure 4–13.

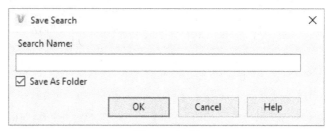

Figure 4–13

3. By default, the **Save As Folder** option is selected. It saves the search as a folder in the *My Search Folders* area so that it can be quickly accessed later.
4. Click **OK** to finish saving the search.

Save a Quick Search

To save a Quick Search, click ˅ (Show search options menu) and select **Save Search** as shown in Figure 4–14.

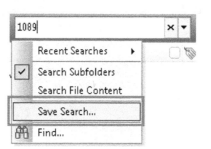

Figure 4–14

Save a Query Builder Search

To save a search from Query Builder, click **Options** and select **Save Search**, as shown in Figure 4–15.

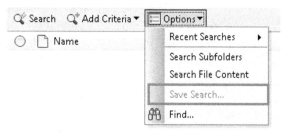

Figure 4–15

My Search Folders

Searches saved with the **Save As Folder** option selected display in the *My Search Folders* area in the Navigation pane in the Autodesk Vault software, as shown in Figure 4–16.

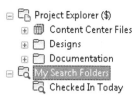

Figure 4–16

To display a search, select the required search folder name in the *My Search Folders* area. The results display in the Main table. A **Find** can also be performed on a search folder to narrow the results.

Run a Saved Search

You can use the Open Saved Search dialog box to run searches that were not saved in the *My Search Folders* area. Select **File>Open Search** in the Find dialog box and then select a saved search in the Open Saved Search dialog box, as shown in Figure 4–17.

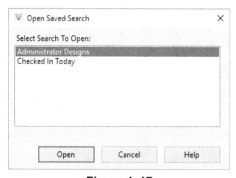

Figure 4–17

How To: Run a Saved Search

You can also click

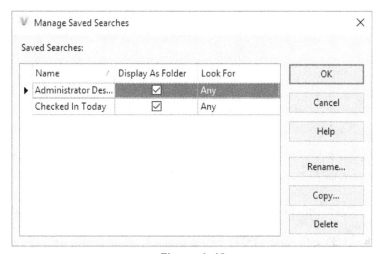 (Open Search) in the toolbar.

1. In the Find dialog box, select **File>Open Search**.
2. In the Open Saved Search dialog box, select the saved search from the list.
3. Click **Open** to execute the search. The search results display in the Find dialog box. The dialog box switches to the tab in which the save was created: *Basic* or *Advanced*.

Manage Saved Searches

You can organize your saved searches in the Manage Saved Searches dialog box. You can rename, copy, and delete saved searches. You can also control whether the saved search displays as a folder in the *My Saved Searches* area.

How To: Modify a Saved Search

1. In the Find dialog box, select **File>Manage Saved Searches**. The Manage Saved Searches dialog box opens as shown in Figure 4–18.

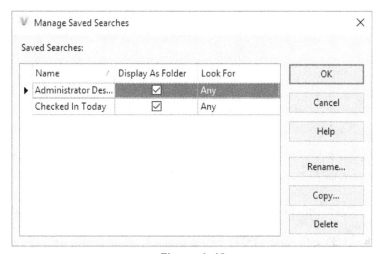

Figure 4–18

*If a search is saved as a search folder, you can also rename the search in the Search Folder list in the Navigation pane by right-clicking and selecting **Rename**.*

2. Perform the following tasks as required:
   - To rename a search, select the search name and click **Rename...**. Enter the new name in the Rename Search dialog box and click **OK**.
   - To copy a search, select the search name in the Manage Saved Searches dialog box and click **Copy...**. Enter the new name and click **OK**.
   - To remove the search from the *My Search Folders* area, clear the **Display As Folder** option.
3. Click **OK** to save the changes and close the Manage Saved Searches dialog box.

Edit Search

You can edit the saved search criteria in the Find dialog box or *My Search Folders* area.

How To: Edit a Saved Search from the Find Dialog Box

1. In the Find dialog box, select **File>Open Search**.
2. In the Open Saved Search dialog box, select the saved search from the list.
3. Click **Open** and make your changes.
4. Click 🖫 (Save Current Search) to save the search with your changes.

How To: Edit a Saved Search from *My Search Folders* Area

1. In *My Search Folders* area, right-click on your saved search and select **Edit Saved Search**, as shown in Figure 4–19.

Figure 4–19

2. The Find dialog box opens with the saved search selected.
3. Make the required changes and click 🖫 (Save Current Search) to save the search with the changes.

Deleting a Saved Search

If a search is saved as a search folder, you can delete the search from the *My Search Folder* area in the Navigation pane or in the Manage Saved Searches dialog box. You are prompted to confirm the deletion of the selected saved search.

How To: Delete a Saved Search

*In the My Search Folder area, right-click and select **Delete**.*

1. In the Find dialog box, select **File>Manage Saved Searches**.
2. In the Manage Saved Searches dialog box, select the search that you want to delete.
3. Click **Delete**.
4. In the Warning box, click **Yes** to confirm the deletion.
5. In the Manage Saved Searches dialog box, click **OK** to save the changes and close the Manage Saved Searches dialog box.

4.7 Reports

There are a number of default report templates available in the Autodesk Vault software. You can use these templates to create Reports. The following lists a few ways to access the Report functionality.

- In the Find dialog box, when Search Results display, click **Report**, as shown in Figure 4–20.

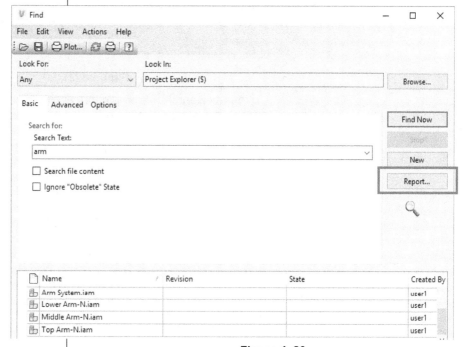

Figure 4–20

- With a folder selected in the Navigation pane, click **Report** on the toolbar, as shown in Figure 4–21. You can also use this button if the folder is selected in the Main table.

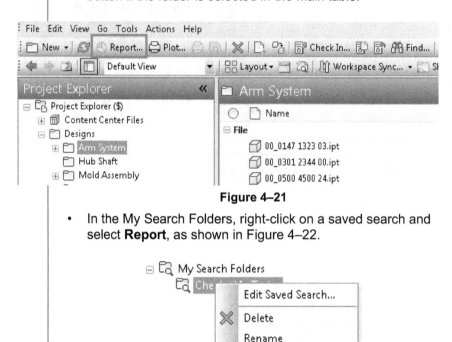

Figure 4–21

- In the My Search Folders, right-click on a saved search and select **Report**, as shown in Figure 4–22.

Figure 4–22

Practice 4a | Searches

Practice Objectives

- Search using a **Quick Search**, **Basic Find**, and **Advanced Find** operation.
- Search file contents.

In this practice, you run a variety of searches to locate files in the database. Each search will produce a view of the database that contains only the files that meet the search criteria. You will also verify the search results and search the file contents.

Task 1 - Search using a Quick Search.

In this task, you locate all files in the vault that contain the word **plan** in their file properties.

1. In Autodesk Vault, log in as **administrator** (no password) and select Project Explorer ($) in the Navigation pane.

2. In the *Quick Search* field, type **plan**, as shown in Figure 4–23.

Figure 4–23

3. Press <Enter>. The search results appear as shown in Figure 4–24.

Figure 4–24

One of the files, LANDSCAPE PLAN-M.dwg, shows the word **plan** in its file name. However, three files, **1STARCH-M.dwg**, **1STLIGHT-M.dwg**, and **1STELEC-M.dwg**, do not.

4. To find what file property in **1STARCH-M.dwg**, for example, contains the word **plan** and to validate the search results, select the file and view the Properties grid.

---

5. The word **plan** exists in the Title, Keywords, and Comments properties as shown in Figure 4–25.

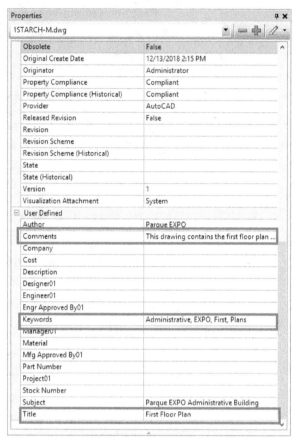

Figure 4–25

Task 2 - Search using the Advanced Find dialog box.

In this task, you want to find all files in the vault where the file property called Title contains the value of **first**. You run a Basic Find with the keyword **first** to see its results. You then run the search again using the Advanced Find search. Compare the results to identify the benefits of using each method.

1. In Autodesk Vault, click **Tools>Find**.

2. Select the Project Explorer ($) as the folder to be searched.

3. Select the *Basic* tab.

4. Type the word **first** in the text field and press <Enter> to execute the search.

5. Several files display in the search results. To filter the list to show only files where the Title file property contains **first**, use Advanced Find.

6. Select the *Advanced* tab.

7. Select **Title** as the property, **contains** as the condition, and type **first** as the value.

8. Select **Add** to add the criteria.

9. Select **Find Now** to execute the search. The search results list now show a shorter list.

10. Close the Find dialog box.

Task 3 - Perform a full content search.

In this task, you perform a Quick Search which includes searching the file contents to find a file that contains the word **cloth**.

1. Select Project Explorer ($) in the Navigation pane.

2. In the Quick Search bar, click ▾ (Show search options menu) and select **Search File Content**, as shown in Figure 4–26.

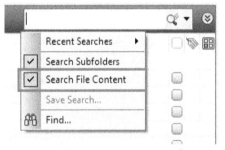

Figure 4–26

3. Type **cloth** in the Search field and press <Enter>. The search result displays the file, **assembly instructions.txt**.

4. View the file to confirm that the word **cloth** is in it.

5. Close the file.

Practice 4b

Saved Searches

Practice Objectives

- Save a search.
- Run a saved search.
- Modify a saved search.
- Delete a saved search.
- Save a search in My Search Folders.

In this practice, you will create several saved searches so that you can run them later for quick access to files that meet the search criteria. You will also modify a saved search, save a search in My Search Folders, and delete a saved search.

Task 1 - Save a search.

In this task, you create and save a search with multiple criteria, that locates all files that belong to the Parque Expo project.

1. Open the Find dialog box and select the *Advanced* tab to start a new search.

2. Add the criteria, **Subject contains Parque** and **Comments contains Parque**, as shown in Figure 4–27.

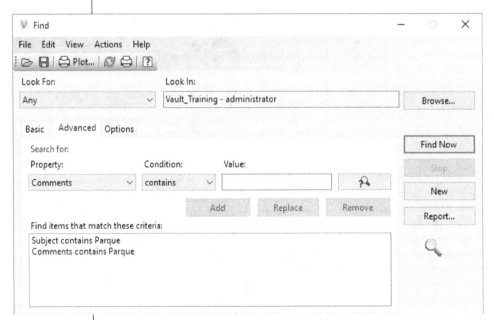

Figure 4–27

3. Click **Find Now**.

4. Click **File>Save Search**.

5. Type **All Parque Expo Files** as the Search Name.

6. Clear the **Save As Folder** option.

7. Click **OK**. Your search is saved in the following location: *C:\Users\[Username]\AppData\Roaming\Autodesk\ VaultCommon\Servers\Services_Security_*\localhost\ Vaults\[Vault_name]\Searches*

Task 2 - Run a saved search.

In this task, you run the saved search called **All Parque Expo Files**.

1. In the Find dialog box, click **File>Open Search**.

2. Select **All Parque Expo Files** and then select **Open** to run the search.

Task 3 - Modify a saved search.

In this task, you modify the **All Parque Expo Files** saved search you created. You modify the search to display it as a search folder and rename it to be **Parque Expo Project**.

1. In the Find dialog box, click **File>Manage Saved Searches**.

2. Select the **All Parque Expo Files** search and click **Rename**. Type **Parque Expo Project** as the new Search Name and click **OK**.

3. Select the **Display As Folder** option.

4. Click **OK** to save the changes and to display the **Parque Expo Project** search folder in the Navigation pane, under My Search Folders, as shown in Figure 4–28.

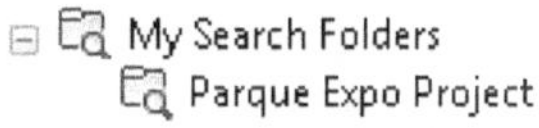

Figure 4–28

Task 4 - Delete the search for Parque Expo Project.

In this task, you delete a saved search.

1. In the Find dialog box, select **File>Manage Saved Searches**.

2. Select the **Parque Expo Project** search.

3. Click **Delete** and **Yes** to confirm the deletion.

4. Click **OK** to complete the deletion and close the Manage Saved Searches window.

5. Close the Find window.

*You can also delete a saved search by right-clicking the search name in the My Search Folders list and clicking the **Delete**.*

Task 5 - Create a saved search for Checked In Today using the Query Builder.

In this task, you will create a saved search using a date property using the Query Builder, and then save it to *My Search Folders*.

1. Click ⊗ (Expand the query builder) next to the Quick Search.

2. Select Project Explorer ($) in the Navigation pane to search from the root folder. The Query Builder displays as shown in Figure 4–29.

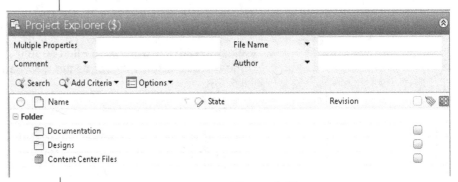

Figure 4–29

3. Click **Add Criteria** and select **Checked In**, as shown in Figure 4–30.

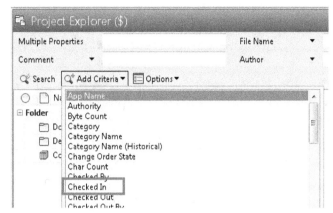

Figure 4–30

4. Expand the Checked In drop-down list as shown in Figure 4–31.

Figure 4–31

5. Select today's date from the calendar and click **Search**. The search results display.

6. Click **Options** and select **Save Search**, as shown in Figure 4–32.

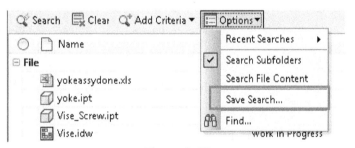

Figure 4–32

7. For the *Search Name*, enter **Checked In Today**.

8. Ensure that the **Save As Folder** option is selected, as shown in Figure 4–33.

Figure 4–33

9. Click **OK**.

10. In *My Search Folders*, select the **Checked In Today** search to view the results in the Main table.

Task 6 - Edit Checked In Today saved search.

---

1. Under *My Search Folders*, right-click **Checked In Today** and select **Edit Saved Search...**, as shown in Figure 4–34.

Figure 4–34

2. Highlight the criteria, then change the Condition to **Today** and click **Replace**, as shown in Figure 4–35.

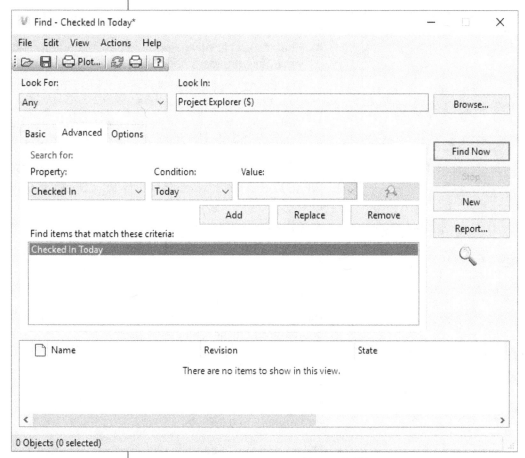

Figure 4–35

3. Click (Save) to save the changes. Now the saved search can be used on any day to view what files have been checked in on that day.

Chapter Review Questions

1. How does the Basic Find search work?

   a. Enables you to navigate the folder structure to find and view design folders and files.

   b. The search locates the files and objects that match the specified file property criteria.

   c. The search locates any file or object in the vault that contains the search string in any of the file properties.

   d. All of the above.

2. What is not a valid search operator for a Basic or Advanced Find?

   a. *

   b. ?

   c. &

   d. NOT

3. What does the Advanced Find enable you to specify to refine your search? (Select all that apply.)

   a. Property Condition (e.g., is, <, >, etc.).

   b. Property Name

   c. Property Value

   d. Location in vault

4. Where can saved searches be executed? (Select all that apply.)

   a. In the **Actions** menu.

   b. *My Search Folders* in the Navigation Pane.

   c. *My Shortcuts* in the Navigation Pane.

   d. In the Find dialog box, select **File>Open Search**.

5. Custom properties can be selected as search criteria.

   a. True

   b. False

Command Summary

Button	Command	Location
🔍 Find...	Find	• **Standard toolbar**
📂	Open Search	• **Find dialog box:** Toolbar
💾	Save Current Search	• **Find dialog box:** Toolbar

Working with Non-CAD Files

When you get and check out files from the Autodesk® Vault software, the vault server downloads copies of the files from the vault to your working folder to make changes. Therefore, you are never directly making changes to the master copies. When viewing files, the server also downloads copies of the files to your working folder. These files are read-only until they are checked out. A file can only be checked out by one user at a time. After changes are made, the file is checked back into the vault.

Learning Objectives in This Chapter

- Differentiate between the functions and procedures of the Get, Check Out, and Undo Check Out operations.
- Modify a checked out non-CAD file and then upload it to the vault using the Check In operation.
- Retrieve the latest version and previous version of a file.
- Differentiate between prompt and dialog box settings for streamlining the file check out and check in processes.
- Differentiate between the file status (vault status) icons, including the differences in their descriptions and required actions.

5.1 Get and Check Out

A file is checked out from the vault so that only one user can perform changes to the file. While the file is checked out, other users cannot modify the checked out files while they are in your control. They can only retrieve a read-only copy of the files until you perform a check in. Checking out temporarily increments the version of the file in the vault (e.g., a file at Version 1 becomes Version 2 on check out). After the changes to the file have been completed, you can check the file back into the vault server, where it remains at the incremented version (e.g., Version 2) and is available again for other users to check out and modify. Figure 5–1 shows a file that is crossed out, indicating that the file is checked out to another user, and a file that you currently have checked out as indicated by the checkmark. In both those cases, you have downloaded the copy locally as indicated by the circle.

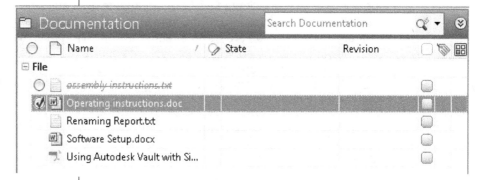

Figure 5–1

One of three options can be used to check out a file: **Get**, **Check Out**, or **Open**.

Get

The **Get** option is used to download a specified version of a file or files to a working folder. You can also choose to check out the file(s).

How To: Check Out a File Using the Get Option

1. Locate the files or use the search tools to locate the required files.

Use <Ctrl> to select multiple files.

2. In the Main table or search results list, select the files to check out, right-click, and select **Get**. The Get dialog box opens showing a *Checkout Count* of **0** and *Download Count* of **1**, as shown in Figure 5–2.

Figure 5–2

3. Click (Expand to show details). The expanded view of the Get dialog box displays, as shown in Figure 5–3.

By default, the Get dialog box is collapsed. If you want the dialog box to stay expanded every time you open it,

click ⬚ (Select the pin to lock the detail view).

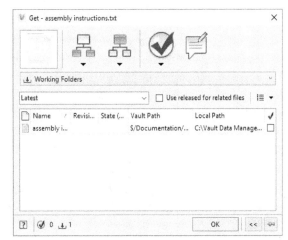

Figure 5–3

*By default, the **Get** command downloads a read-only version of the file to the working folder without checking it out.*

4. If you want to check out the file, click the checkbox in the Check Out column, as shown in Figure 5–4. You can also

click ✅ (Check Out Files) to automatically add the checkmark.

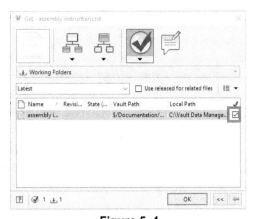

Figure 5–4

5. Click one or more of the buttons or options that are described as follows:

Option	Description
☑ Dependents ☐ Attachments ☑ Include Library Files	Click (Include Children) to automatically include specified children files when you check an object out of the vault. Click the drop-down arrow to select the children types that are included when the button is selected.
◉ No Parents ○ Direct Parents ○ All Parents ☑ Related Documentation	Click (Include Parents) to automatically include specified parent files when you check an object out of the vault. Click the drop-down arrow to select the parent types, if any, that are included when the button is clicked.
○ Source Selection ◉ All Files	Click (Check Out) to automatically select all of the objects listed for check out. Click the drop-down arrow to change your settings from *All Files* to **Source Selection** if you only want to select the files that were initially highlighted in the main view when you opened the Get/Check Out dialog box.
Working Folders / Working Folders / Working Folders - Force Overwrite / None / Browse...	Expand the *Working Folders* drop-down list to select the default working folder or browse to another folder in which to store the local copies of the objects that you download. You can also select **None** to not have a working folder.
Modify the second procedure	Click (Comments) to add a description or a comment stating why you are checking out the file, such as for a required modification.
Latest ▼	Set to **Latest** to copy the latest version of the file from the vault to the working folder. You can also select any past revisions that are available in the vault.
☐ Use released for related files	Select this checkbox to get the released versions of all selected related files.

6. Review the files that are going to be checked out. The display can be controlled using the view icons, as shown in Figure 5–5.

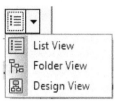

Figure 5–5

7. Click  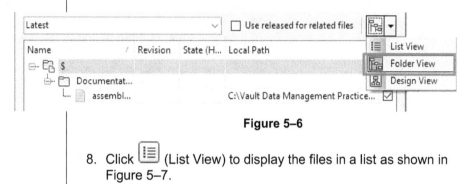 (Folder View) to display the selected files in a Folder view, as shown in Figure 5–6.

Figure 5–6

8. Click ▤ (List View) to display the files in a list as shown in Figure 5–7.

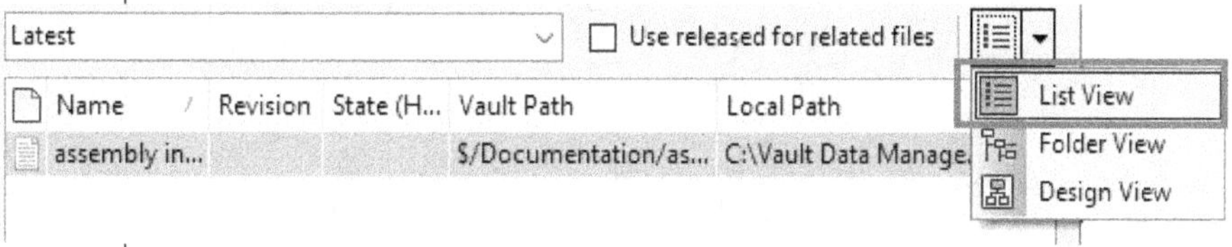

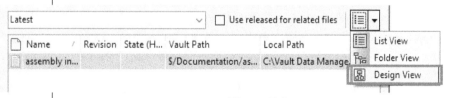

Figure 5–7

9. Click ▦ (Design View) to display the files to be checked out without their folder structure as shown in Figure 5–8.

Figure 5–8

10. If you want to exclude any of the displayed files from the selection that are going to be checked out, clear the check box next to their filenames.

11. Click **OK** to complete, which downloads the files to the working folder.

Check Out

You can use **Check Out** to perform a quick check out on a file. It bypasses the Get dialog box and always checks out the latest version of the file. Note that the file is checked out but not downloaded to the working folder.

How To: Check Out a File Using the Check Out Option

1. Locate the files or use the search tools to locate the required files.

Use <Ctrl> to select multiple files.

2. In the Main table or search results list, select the files to check out, right-click, and select **Check Out**. The files are immediately checked out but not downloaded, as indicated by the bold blue file name without a circle beside it, as shown in Figure 5–9.

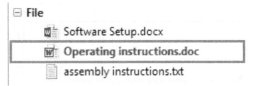

Figure 5–9

Open

You can use **Open** to check out the latest version of a file.

How To: Check Out a File Using the Open Option

1. Locate the file or search for the required files using the search tools.
2. In the Main table or search results list, select the file that you want to check out, right-click, and select **Open**. You are immediately prompted to check out the file, as shown in Figure 5–10.

You can also select ***File>Open*** *or press <Ctrl>+<O>.*

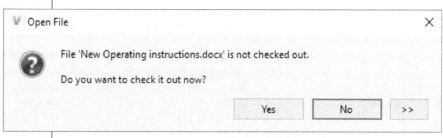

Figure 5–10

3. Click **Yes** to check out the latest version of the file and open it in the associated application. It is also downloaded to the working folder.

5.2 Undo Check Out

If you have checked out a file but do not need to make changes to it, you can perform an **Undo Check Out** operation. This cancels the change operation to the selected file in the vault and your working folder, effectively setting the file back to the way it was before the check out operation. An **Undo Check Out** operation can also be performed on multiple files, or on a folder and all of its contents. Only the user who checked out the file can undo the check out.

How To: Undo a Check Out

1. Locate the files or search for the required files using the available search tools.
2. Select the files in the Main table or search results list, right-click, and select **Undo Check Out**. The Undo Check Out dialog box opens as shown in Figure 5–11.
   - You can also select **Actions>Undo Check Out** or click

      (Undo Check Out) in the Standard toolbar.

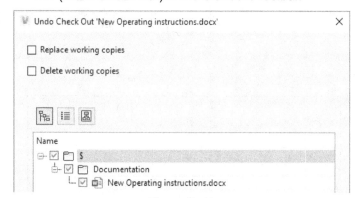

Figure 5–11

3. Select **Replace working copies** if you want the file in your working folder to return to the state it was in before you checked it out.
4. Select **Delete working copies** if you want the file in your working folder to be removed. This is a recommended best practice to ensure that you are always working with the latest version of the file.
5. Click (Settings) to control the inclusion settings of the children, parents, and related documentation of the selected files. The children are included by default.
6. Click **OK** to complete the operation.

Multiple objects can be selected using <Ctrl>.

*To perform an **Undo Check Out** operation on an entire folder, select the folder, right-click, and select **Undo Check Out**.*

5.3 Modifying Non-CAD Files

When a non-CAD file has been checked out, it can be modified and then checked in again. This enables you to use the version functionality on non-CAD files.

How To: Modify a Checked Out Non-CAD File

1. In the working folder select a file and open it in its associated application.
   - If the **Open** option was used, the application is opened automatically.
2. Make the required changes and save them. The changes are saved to your local working folder.
3. Check in the file.

5.4 Check In

After modifications are made to the file in the local working folder, the file can be checked back into the vault so that others can access the file with the latest changes.

How To: Check In a File

1. Locate the files or search for the required files using the search tools.

Multiple objects can be selected using <Ctrl>.

2. In the Main table or search results list, select the files to check in, right-click, and select **Check In**. The Check In dialog box opens as shown in Figure 5–12.
   - You can also select **Actions>Check In** or click ▣ (Check In) in the Standard toolbar.

Figure 5–12

3. Select **Keep files checked out** if you want to check the files back out immediately after checking them in.
4. Select **Delete working copies** to remove the local copy after the file is checked into the vault.
5. Click ▣ (Settings) to control the inclusion settings of the children, parents, and related documentation of the selected files. By default, the children are included.
6. In the *Enter comments to include...* area, enter any notes regarding this version.
7. Click **OK** to complete the operation.

5.5 File Versions

In the Get dialog box, you can download the latest version of the file to get or check out. You can also revert to a previous version, if required.

- Deleting the local copy of your files to ensure that you are always working with the latest version is a recommended best practice.

Latest Version

In the Get dialog box, use **Latest** to download the most current version of the selected files to your local working folder.

How To: Get the Latest Version of a File

1. Select the file, right-click, and select **Get**. The Get dialog box opens as shown in Figure 5–13.

   - You can also select **Actions>Get** or click 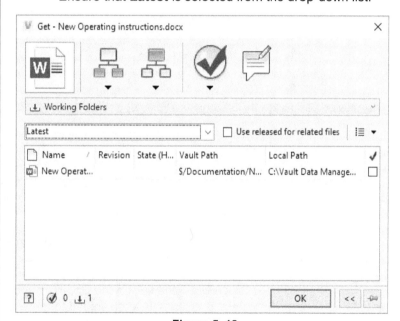 (Get) in the Standard toolbar.
   - Ensure that **Latest** is selected from the drop-down list.

Figure 5–13

2. Click **Include Children** or **Include Parents** to control the inclusion settings of the children and parents of the selected file.
3. Click **OK** to complete the operation.

Previous Revision

There might be times when you want to revert back to a previous revision of a file. To do this, in the Get dialog box, in the drop-down list, select the revision to download to your local working folder. Open the files from your local working folder.

Previous Versions

There might be times when you want to revert back to a previous version of a file.

How To: Revert to a Previous Version of a File

1. Select a file, right-click on it, and select **Check Out**.
2. Select the *History* tab.
3. Select the **Show all versions** checkbox.
4. Select the file version that you would like to download, as shown in Figure 5–14.

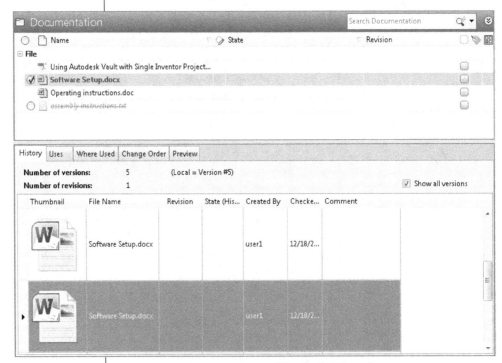

Figure 5–14

5. Right-click on the file and select **Get**.
6. Click **OK** to download to the working folder.
7. Click **Yes** if prompted to overwrite the working folder file with the file from the vault.
8. Now you can open the file from the working folder in the associated application and make any changes. Once it is checked back in to the Vault, it will be the latest version.

5.6 Managing Prompts and Dialog Boxes

To streamline the workflow process, you can manage the prompt and dialog box defaults that are related to lifecycle operations. In addition, you can specify which operations are performed automatically without prompting for input.

In the Autodesk Vault software, select **Tools>Options** to open the Options dialog box, as shown in Figure 5–15.

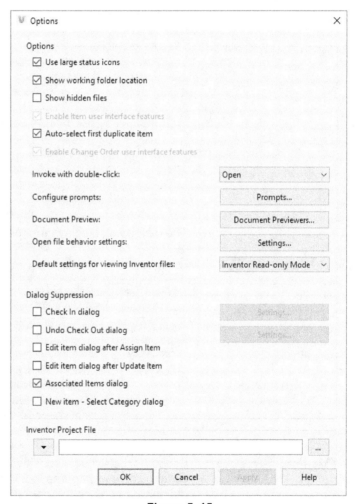

Figure 5–15

Prompts

To manage the default prompt settings, click **Prompts...** in the Options dialog box. The Manage Prompts dialog box opens as shown in Figure 5–16.

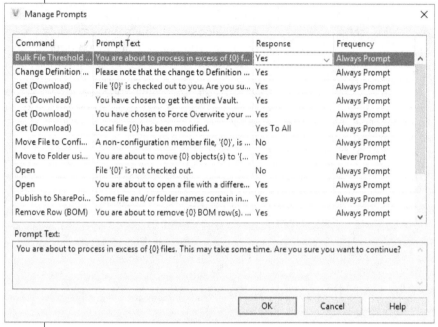

Figure 5–16

The dialog box displays four columns:

Command	Displays the command name.
Prompt Text	Displays the text that is displayed in the Warning box related to the selected command.
Response	Set the default response to the prompt.
Frequency	Set the frequency at which the prompt displays. • Select **Always prompt** to open its dialog box each time. This is the default. • Select **Never prompt** to use the answer that you select for the response as the new default.

Dialog Boxes

Dialog boxes associated with lifecycle operations can be customized and suppressed. If a dialog box is suppressed, it is not displayed when the operation is performed. This streamlines and automates the workflow process. In the *Dialog Suppression* area, select the dialog box option that you want to modify and click **Settings...** to open the related Settings dialog box.

The list of dialog boxes and their associated settings include those shown in Figure 5–17 and Figure 5–18:

Settings for Check In dialog box

Figure 5–17

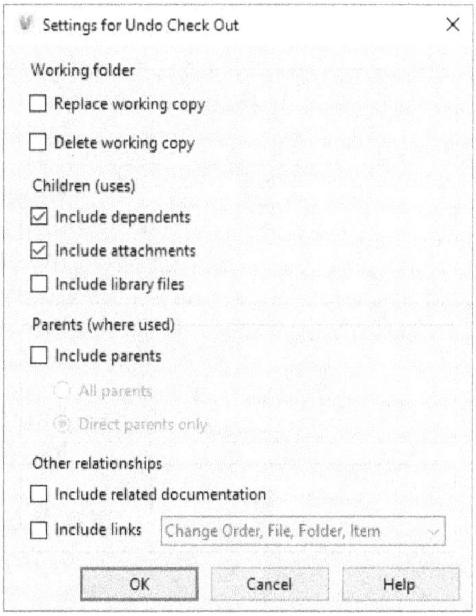

Settings for Undo Check Out dialog box

Figure 5–18

Document Preview

Use the *Document Preview* area to control document previews. Click **Document Previewers...** to open the Document Previewer Options dialog box, shown in Figure 5–19. Toggle a specific previewer by selecting the checkbox next to the option.

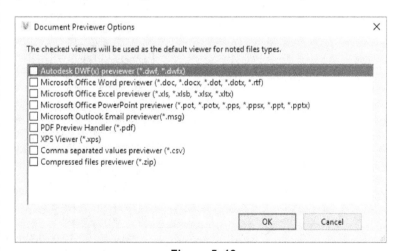

Figure 5–19

5.7 File Status

The status of a file in the vault, shown with vault status icons, status fonts, and modifiers, displays in the Autodesk Vault software and in the Autodesk Inventor Vault Browser.

- **Black/Normal font:** The file is not checked out.

- **Blue/Bold:** The file is checked out to you. An asterisk will display at the end of the file name if the file has been modified but not been saved.

- **Gray/Italic/Strikethrough:** The file is checked out to another user.

- **Vault Status Modifier (+):** The file's edits have been saved locally.

Vault Status Icons

Icon	Description	Required Action
No icon	Indicates that the file is in the vault in a checked in state and that you do not have a local copy.	The file is available to be checked out, or a local copy can be retrieved using the **Get** command.
○ **(empty)**	The file is in the vault in a checked in state and the read-only version you are working on is the same as the one in the vault (also known as *Latest Version* or *leading version of the leading revision* of the file).	The read-only file is available to be checked out.
● **(green)**	The file is in the vault in a checked in state, but the version you are working on is newer than the latest version in the vault.	Typically means that your local file was changed without checking it out. To save any changes,
◉	The file is checked out to you and the version you are working on is the same as the one in the vault (also known as *Latest Version*).	Use **Check In** to check the file back into the vault or select **Undo Check Out** to cancel any changes.
△	The local copy is a historical revision of the leading revision in the vault.	=
◉ **(green)**	The file is checked out to you but the version you are working on is newer than the latest version in the vault.	Typically means you made changes to the file since it was checked out but have not yet checked it back in.

↺	The file is not in the vault.	Use **Check In** to add the file to the vault.
⟳	The local copy does not match the latest version in the vault.	Use the **Refresh from Vault** command to obtain the latest version of the file.
🔒	The file is locked and the local copy is up-to-date.	
🔒	The file is locked and the local copy is not up-to-date.	
ⓘ	There has been an unexpected revision with the file, or the status could not be determined.	Review the tooltip for the action required.

Practice 5a

Modifying a Text File

Practice Objectives

- Locate and check out a text file.
- Modify a text file and check it back into the vault.
- Check out the file as another user.
- View the Vault Status and display the file's Version History.

In this practice, you will make modifications to an assembly instructions file. You will locate the file, check it out, make modifications, and then check it back into the vault. You will then check out the file as another user and as the original user, display the file's history.

Task 1 - Locate, get, and check out a text file.

1. In the Autodesk Vault software, log in as **user1** without a password.

2. Locate the file **assembly instructions.txt**.

3. Select the file, right-click, and select **Get**.

4. In the Get dialog box, click ⟩⟩ (Expand to show details) and ensure that it is set to **Latest**.

5. In the *Check Out* area, select the Check Out checkbox for **assembly instructions.txt**, or click ✓ (Check Out Files) to automatically select the file for check out. The dialog box updates showing that one file will be checked out and one file will be downloaded, as shown in Figure 5–20.

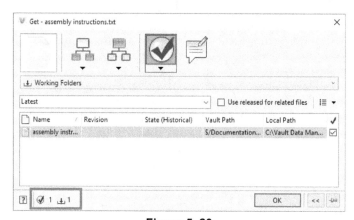

Figure 5–20

6. Click 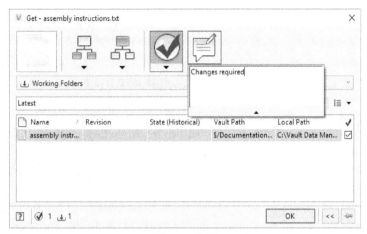 (Comments). In the text field, type **Changes required** as shown in Figure 5–21.

Figure 5–21

7. Click **OK**.

8. The Main table updates. Note that the vault status icon has updated to display ⟨✓⟩ and that the filename has a blue bold font. The file is checked out to you and the version you are working on is the same as the one in the vault (also known as the *Latest Version* or *leading version* of the leading revision of the file).The comments entered are also shown in the preview pane, as shown in Figure 5–22.

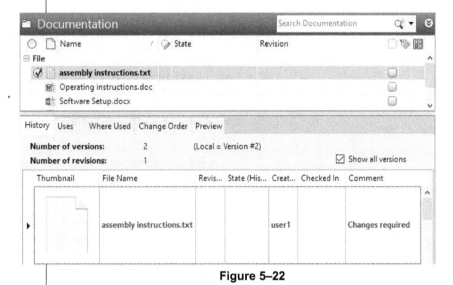

Figure 5–22

Task 2 - Open the text file and edit it.

In this task, you will open the text file in Notepad for modification.

1. Select **assembly instructions.txt**, right-click, and select **Open** to launch the Notepad application.

2. Edit the file in Notepad by adding the text: **4. Insert the 4 bolts into the holes.**

3. Save the file and exit Notepad.

4. In the Main table, refresh the display. The vault status icon updates to display a green circle with a checkmark 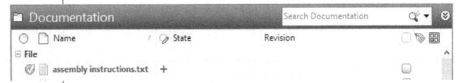, indicating that the file is still checked out to you and that the version you are working on, in the working folder, is newer than the latest version in the vault. There is also a plus sign (+) in the Vault Status Modifier column, indicating the file's edits have been saved locally, as shown in Figure 5–23.

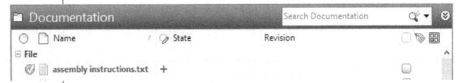

Figure 5–23

Task 3 - Check in the document.

In this task, you will release ownership of the file by checking it back into the vault. This is done to enable other users to view your modifications and for you to add comments.

1. Select **assembly instructions.txt**, right-click, and select **Check In**.

2. Select **Delete working copies**. This is a recommended best practice.

3. In the *Enter comments to include...* area, type **Added step 4.** as shown in Figure 5–24. Click **OK**.

Figure 5–24

Task 4 - Check out the document as another user.

A co-worker now needs to add to the instructions.

1. Log out of the Autodesk Vault software by selecting **File>Log Out**.

2. Log back in as **user2** without a password.

3. Locate the **assembly instructions.txt** file, right-click and select **Get**.

4. Click (Check Out Files) to select the file for check out.

5. For the comment, type **Further modifications required** and click **OK** to perform the check out.

6. Log out of the Autodesk Vault software.

Task 5 - View vault status and display version history.

In this task, you will log back in as user1 and view the vault status and version history of the assembly instructions file.

1. Log in to the Autodesk Vault software as **user1**.

2. Locate the **assembly instructions.txt** file. Note that the file is crossed out, indicating that the file is checked out by someone else, as shown in Figure 5–25.

Figure 5–25

3. Select the file, right-click, and click **Get**. Click  (Expand to show details). Note that the **Check Out** option is not available in the Get dialog box because the file is checked out by **user2**, as shown in Figure 5–26.

Figure 5–26

4. Close the Get dialog box.

5. In the Preview pane, select the *History* tab to view the version history, as shown in Figure 5–27. Select **Show all versions** to show the version history.

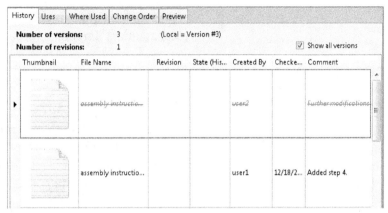

Figure 5–27

Chapter Review Questions

1. When a file is checked out, no other users can modify it because it is set to a read-only status in the Autodesk Data Management Server.

   a. True

   b. False

2. What does an **Undo Check Out** operation do?

   a. Cancels the change operation to the selected file, increasing the version of the file.

   b. Cancels the change operation to the selected file, deleting the file from the database.

   c. Cancels the change operation to the selected file, keeping the file checked out.

   d. Cancels the change operation to the selected file, setting the file back to the way it was before the check out operation.

3. If Version 3 of a file is checked out, modified, checked back in, checked out again, and then an undo check out is performed, what is the version of the file in the database?

   a. 3

   b. 4

   c. 5

   d. 6

4. What are the steps for reverting to a previous version of a file?

    a. Use **Check Out**, and then open the file from the working folder.

    b. Check Out the file. In the file's *History* tab, ensure that the **Show all versions** option is selected, and then select the required version. Right-click, select **Get**, and then click **OK** to download.

    c. Use **Get**, select the previous version from the list, then use the **Open from Vault** command to open the previous version from the vault database.

    d. Use **Get**, select the previous version from the list, then open the file from the working folder.

    e. Use **Get**, select the latest version from the list, then open the file from the working folder.

5. What is the file status of an icon showing a white circle with a checkmark ()?

    a. The file is checked out to you and the version you are working on is the same as the one in the vault.

    b. The file is checked out to you but there is no local copy in the working folder.

    c. The file is checked out by another user and the read-only version you are working on is the same as the one in the vault.

    d. The file is checked out to you but the version you are working on is newer than the latest version in the vault.

Command Summary

Button	Command	Location
	Check In	• **Menu:** Actions>Check In • **Shortcut:** (*right-click on selected file*) • **Standard Toolbar**
	Get	• **Menu:** Actions>Get • **Shortcut:** (*right-click on selected file*) • **Standard Toolbar**
	Check Out	• **Menu:** Actions>Check Out • **Shortcut:** (*right-click on selected file*)
	Undo Check Out	• **Menu:** Actions>Undo Check Out • **Shortcut:** (*right-click on selected file*) • **Standard Toolbar**

Working with AutoCAD Files

As with non-CAD files, the Autodesk® Vault software records the process of change in an AutoCAD file when you use the Autodesk Vault software and Vault Add-in to check out files from the vault. In this chapter, you learn how to use the **Check Out**, **Check In**, and **Undo Check Out** commands. You also learn how to change the lifecycle states and revisions for AutoCAD designs.

Learning Objectives in This Chapter

- Check out AutoCAD files in the AutoCAD software using multiple methods.
- Undo a Check Out operation in the AutoCAD software.
- Modify checked out AutoCAD files and check the files back in to the vault.
- Retrieve a previous version of a file and then open it in the AutoCAD software.
- Change the lifecycle states and create new revisions of AutoCAD files.
- Create PDFs.
- Differentiate between prompt and dialog box settings for streamlining the check out and check in processes for AutoCAD files.

6.1 Check Out AutoCAD Files

A file is checked out to a client from the vault so that only one person can perform changes to the file. While a file is checked out, other users cannot modify the checked out file while they are in your control. They can only retrieve a read-only copy of a file until you check it back in. For AutoCAD files, you can select one of the following four methods to check out the latest version of a file:

- Check out a file using **Open** in the *Vault* tab>Access panel in the AutoCAD software. You will be prompted to check out.

- Check out from the External References palette in AutoCAD.

- Check out a file using the **Open** option in the Autodesk Vault software.You will be prompted to check out.

In the AutoCAD software, after the drawing has been checked out, the window header updates to show the drawing as Checked Out, as shown in Figure 6–1.

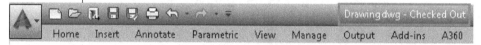

Figure 6–1

Check Out Using Open from Vault

You can use **Open** in the *Vault* tab>Access panel to check out the latest file from the vault when you open it in the AutoCAD software. This is a different function from the standard AutoCAD **Open** command since the file is opened directly from the vault.

How To: Check Out a File in the AutoCAD Software

1. In the *Vault* tab>Access panel, click ![icon] (Open from the vault).
2. In the Select File dialog box, expand **Open**, and select one of the check out options: **Open (Check Out)** or **Open (Check Out All)** as shown in Figure 6–2.

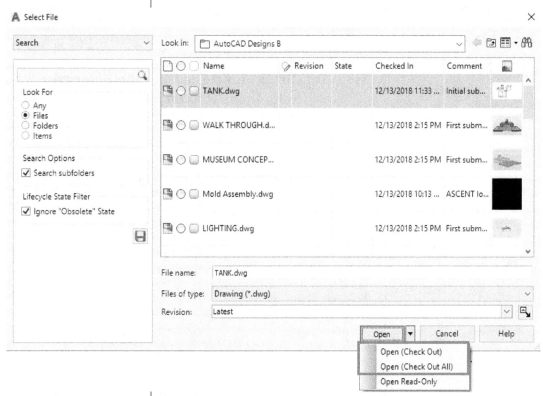

Figure 6–2

If you click **Open** when retrieving an AutoCAD file and the file is available for check out, a Warning box opens prompting you to check the file out, as shown in Figure 6–3.

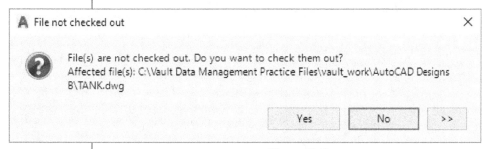

Figure 6–3

Check Out from the External References Palette

If you decide to open the file as read-only from the vault, you can check out the file at any time through the External References palette.

How To: Check Out a File from the External References Palette

1. In the External References palette, right-click the host or XREF and select **Check Out**, as shown in Figure 6–4.

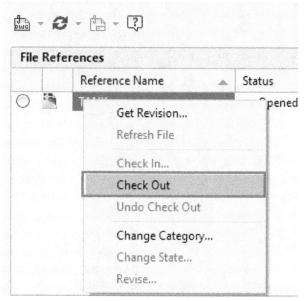

Figure 6–4

Check Out Using Open in Autodesk Vault Client

In the Autodesk Vault software, you can check out the file at any time using the **Open** option when prompted. Using this option you cannot specify which version of the file is being checked out. The latest version is automatically checked out.

How To: Check Out an AutoCAD File Using the Open Option

1. Locate the file or search for the required files using the search tools.
2. In the Main table or search results area, select the file that you want to check out, right-click, and select **Open**, as shown in Figure 6–5.

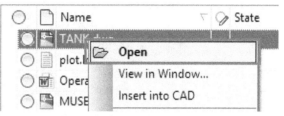

Figure 6–5

3. In the Open File dialog box, select **Yes** to open and check out the file, or **No** to open without checking out the file, as shown in Figure 6–6.

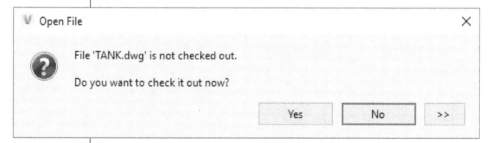

Figure 6–6

6.2 Undo Check Out in AutoCAD

If you have checked out a file but do not need to make changes to it, you can perform an **Undo Check Out** operation. This cancels the change operation to the selected file in the vault and your working folder, effectively setting the file back to how it was before the check out operation. An **Undo Check Out** operation can also be performed on multiple files, or on a folder and all of its contents. Only the user who checked out the file can undo the check out.

For AutoCAD files, the following methods can be used to undo a check out:

- Select (Undo Check Out) in the *Vault* tab>File Status panel within AutoCAD.

- Select the **Undo Check Out** command in the External References palette in AutoCAD.

- In Autodesk Vault, select the file, right-click and select **Undo Check Out**.

How To: Undo a Check Out

1. Using one of the methods, select **Undo Check Out**. The Undo Check Out dialog box opens, as shown in Figure 6–7.

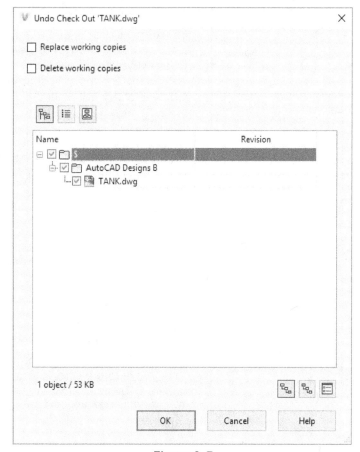

Figure 6–7

2. Select **Replace working copies** if you want to replace the local file with the version that is currently stored in the vault.
3. Select **Delete working copies** if you want the file in your working folder to be removed. This is a recommended best practice to ensure that you are always working with the latest version.
4. Click **Settings...** to control the settings of the children and parents of the selected files.
5. Click **OK**.

6.3 Modifying AutoCAD Files

The vault enables multiple users to access the same design project and work on different portions of the design or XREFs.

For example, user1 can be working on XREF A of a drawing and user2 on XREF B, which is used in the same drawing. They can both retrieve a read-only copy of the host drawing to their working folders and only check out the XREF for modification. If you try to check out a file that has already been checked out to someone else, you will see that Check Out is grayed out and cannot be selected.

If you try to modify a file that has not yet been checked out and is available for check out, a message opens, as shown in Figure 6–8.

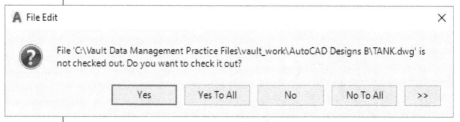

Figure 6–8

After modifications are performed, a file must be saved in AutoCAD before a **Check In** operation can be performed. By default, if you try to close a checked out AutoCAD file without checking it in, the system prompts you to decide whether you want to check in the file.

6.4 Check In AutoCAD Files

After modifications are made to the file in the local working folder and it is saved, the file can be checked back into the vault so that other users can access the file containing the latest changes.

For AutoCAD files, the following methods can be used to check in:

- Select 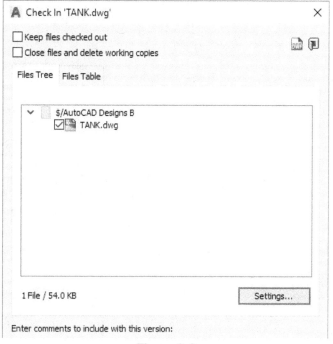 (Check In) in the *Vault* tab>File Status panel within AutoCAD.

- In the External References palette within AutoCAD, select the file, right-click, and select **Check in**.

How To: Check In an AutoCAD File

1. Using one of the methods, select **Check In**. The Check In dialog box opens as shown in Figure 6–9.

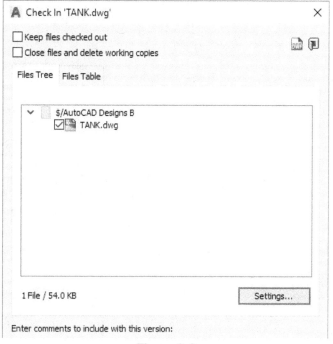

Figure 6–9

2. Select **Keep Files Checked Out** if you want to keep the files checked out for further modifications.

3. Select **Close files and delete working copies** to remove the local copy after the file is checked into the vault. This is a recommended best practice. If required, close the file in the AutoCAD software.

Specifying the file location structure is only available for the first check in operation.

4. Click **Settings** to specify whether or not .DWF files are automatically created and attached to the files by setting the Visualization Attachment options, as shown in Figure 6–10.

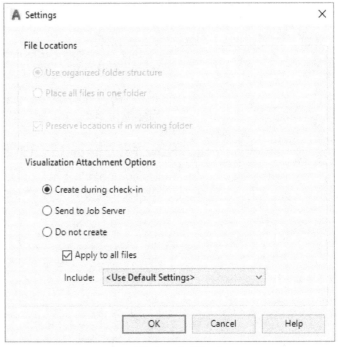

Figure 6–10

5. In the *Enter comments to include...* area, type comments to explain the changes for this version.
6. Click **OK** to complete the operation. The AutoCAD window header now shows the drawing as **Read Only**, as shown in Figure 6–11.

Figure 6–11

6.5 Get Previous Versions in AutoCAD

Note: To retrieve older versions of AutoCAD files from Autodesk Vault, you must be in the Autodesk Vault software and use the **Get** command. It cannot be done directly in the AutoCAD software.

How To: Revert to a Previous Version

1. Select the file, right-click on it, and then select **Check Out**.
2. Select the *History* tab.
3. Select **Show all versions**.
4. Select the version of the file that you would like to download.
5. Right-click on the file and click **Get**.
6. The previous version of the file is shown in the dialog box. Click **OK** to download to the working folder.
7. Click **Yes** when prompted to overwrite the working folder file with the file from the vault, as shown in Figure 6–12.

Figure 6–12

8. Now you can open the file from the working folder in AutoCAD and make any changes. Once it is checked back in to the vault, it will be the latest version.

6.6 Changing Lifecycle States and Next Release/Revision Procedures

Change State

The **Change State** command enables you to change the lifecycle state of a selected object.

How To: Change State

1. Select the objects from the main pane.
2. Click **Change State**, or right-click and select **Change State**.
3. Select a lifecycle definition, if required, and then select the lifecycle state from the drop-down list.
4. Click **Settings** for children and parent options, if required.
5. Type a comment or select from a list of predefined comments.
6. Click **OK**.

The following is a list of predefined Lifecycle States for the Flexible Release Process that is associated with the Engineering Category:

State Name	Description
Work In Progress	Also known as WIP, this state typically involves the editing of the files. By default, the Revision will increment when the state is changed to WIP.
For Review/In Review	In general, no editing is permitted at this state.
Released	Typically read-only access where editing is not permitted.
Obsolete	Designs are no longer active and therefore access is restricted. Typically, no edits can be made.

Change Revision and Revise

The **Change Revision** and **Revise** commands create a new revision of a file or item.

The **Revise** command is found in AutoCAD in the *Vault* tab. The **Change Revision** command is found in Autodesk Vault in the **Actions** menu or toolbar.

When you need to make changes to a file or item that has already been released into production, you must first create a new revision. This protects the integrity of the existing released version, and creates a new version on which to make the changes. When a file is revised, its revision is incremented following a predefined sequence, and the version number is reset to 1.

How To: Create a New Revision in AutoCAD

1. In AutoCAD, open the file you want to revise.
2. In the *Vault* tab, click **Revise**, as shown in Figure 6–13.

Figure 6–13

3. Select one of the format options shown in Figure 6–14.

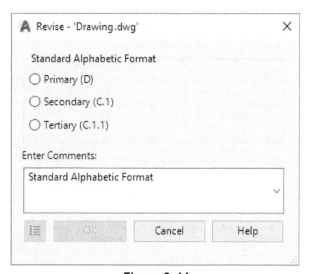

Figure 6–14

4. Click **OK**.

How To: Create a New Revision in Autodesk Vault

1. In Autodesk Vault, select a file and then in the toolbar, select **Change Revision**.
2. In the Select next revision drop-down list, select **Primary**, **Secondary**, or **Tertiary**, as shown in Figure 6–15.

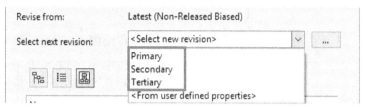

Figure 6–15

3. Click **OK**.

Released Biased

Released Biased is an option that determines if released objects should take priority over unreleased objects. This option can be toggled on and off, as shown in Figure 6–16. The **Released Biased** toggle is also available when opening or attaching AutoCAD files from the Vault.

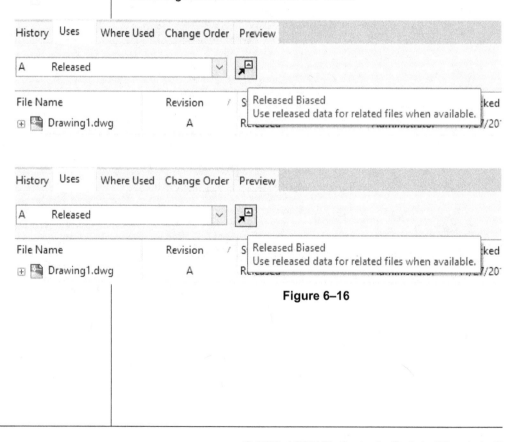

Figure 6–16

6.7 Get Revision

You can retrieve a specific revision of a file, if and when required.

How To: Get a Specific Revision

1. In the AutoCAD software, select **Get Revision**, as shown in Figure 6–17.

Figure 6–17

The Revision drop-down list is also available when opening or placing AutoCAD files in the vault.

2. Select a revision from the Select Revision drop-down list, as shown in Figure 6–18.

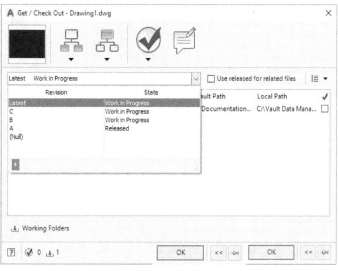

Figure 6–18

3. Click **OK**.

Roll Back Lifecycle State Change

Another method to revert to a previous revision is to undo the revision change using the **Roll Back Lifecycle State Change** command.

How To: Roll Back a File's Lifecycle State

1. Select a file in the main table and select **Actions>Roll Back Lifecycle State Change...**, as shown in Figure 6–19.

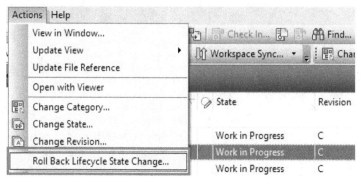

Figure 6–19

2. A window opens describing to which state the file will be rolled back. Click **Yes** to continue and complete the lifecycle state rollback, as shown in Figure 6–20.

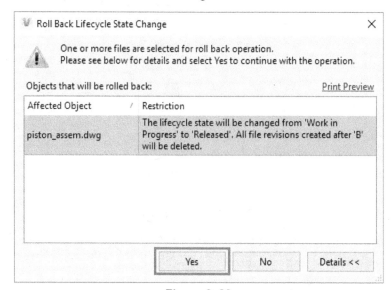

Figure 6–20

6.8 Creating PDFs

You can automatically publish 2D PDF files from your AutoCAD files when releasing your designs at the released state or at any other lifecycle state. You can also manually create a PDF of a 2D CAD file using the **Create PDF** command.

Note: To be able to use the **Create PDF** command, you must have the required access privileges set by your administrator.

By default, PDF files created automatically from 2D files are attached to the 2D design file and can be viewed in the *Uses* tab as an attachment, as shown in Figure 6–21.

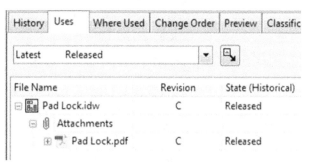

Figure 6–21

How To: Create a PDF Manually Using the Create PDF Command

1. Select the 2D file in the main table, and then select **Actions> Create PDF** or right-click and select **Create PDF**.
2. The PDF is created. The location of the PDF depends on the setting for the PDF Publish Location set by the administrator. The three options are:
   - **Disable PDF Publish Folder Location**: Disables to publish PDF files locally. Automatically generated PDF files are still created in the Vault Client.
   - **Flat List:** Select to store all the PDF files in a single folder on the local computer.
   - **Duplicate Vault Folder Structure:** Select to store local copies of the files in a folder structure that duplicates the structure used in Vault Client.

*By default automatically generated PDF files are hidden. Select **Tools> Options** to display hidden files.*

6.9 Managing Prompts and Dialog Boxes

To streamline the workflow process, you can customize the prompt and dialog box defaults that are related to **Check In**, **Check Out**, and **Undo Check Out** operations. In addition, you can specify which operations are performed automatically without prompting for your input.

In AutoCAD, in the *Vault* tab>File Status panel, click (Vault Options) to open the Options dialog box, as shown in Figure 6–22.

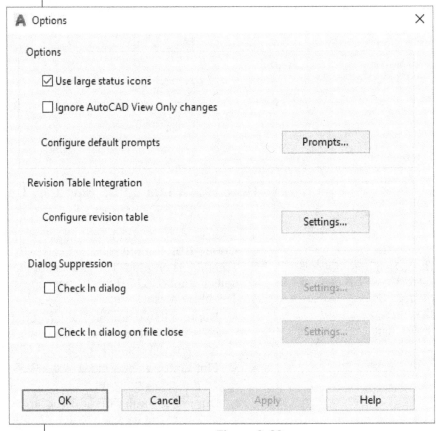

Figure 6–22

Prompts

To manage the default prompt settings, click **Prompts...** in the *Options* area. The Manage Prompts dialog box opens as shown in Figure 6–23.

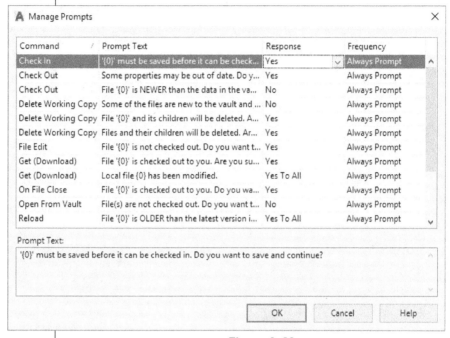

Figure 6–23

The dialog box displays four columns:

Command	Displays the command name.
Prompt Text	Displays the text that is displayed in the Warning box related to the selected command.
Response	Set the default response to the prompt.
Frequency	Set the frequency at which the prompt displays. • **Always Prompt** - This is the default prompt setting. Leave the default setting as is, if you require the prompt dialog box to display each time. • **Never Prompt** - Set it to Never Prompt, if you require automatic processing of the prompt request and do not want the prompt dialog box to display. The response you select will determine how the prompt will be automatically processed.

Dialog Boxes

Dialog boxes associated with vault operations such as Check In can be customized with default settings and suppressed. When the operation is performed, no dialog box opens, therefore streamlining and automating the workflow. In the *Dialog Suppression* area, select the dialog box option that you want to modify and click **Settings...** to open the related Settings dialog box.

The list of dialog boxes and their associated settings include the Check In dialog box and Check In dialog box on file close, as shown in Figure 6–24 and Figure 6–25.

Settings for Check In dialog box

Figure 6–24

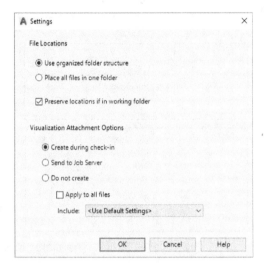

Settings for Check In dialog box on file close

Figure 6–25

Practice 6a

Modifying an AutoCAD Design

Practice Objectives

- Locate and check out an AutoCAD drawing.
- Modify an AutoCAD drawing and check it back into the vault.
- Use the Undo Check Out command to undo the changes made while the drawing was checked out.

In this practice, you check out an AutoCAD drawing, make changes, and then check it back into the vault. You then make some additional changes and use the **Undo Check Out** command to undo your changes.

Task 1 - Open a drawing from the vault.

1. In AutoCAD, click  (Open from the vault) in the *Vault* tab>Access panel.

2. Browse to the *$/AutoCAD Designs B* vault folder and select **WALK THROUGH.dwg**. Select **Open**.

3. Select **Yes** to check out the drawing and select **Yes** to update the properties.

Task 2 - Modify the drawing, save, and check in.

In this task, you make a change to the drawing by removing the fountain. You then save the changes and check back in the drawing.

1. In AutoCAD, select the fountain, and press <Delete> to erase it, as shown in Figure 6–26.

Figure 6–26

2. Save the changes.

3. Open the External References palette to view the vault status icon of a green circle with a checkmark. This indicates that the file saved to the disk is more recent than the one in the vault and is checked out to you, as shown in Figure 6–27.

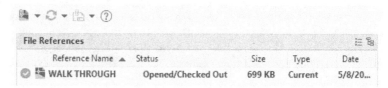

Figure 6–27

4. Hover the cursor over the Vault Status icon to view the tooltip.

5. In the External References palette, select **WALK THROUGH**, right-click, and click **Check In**.

6. Type **Removed fountain** in the Check In dialog box comments area, as shown in Figure 6–28.

Figure 6–28

7. Click **OK**. The drawing remains on screen but is not checked out.

Task 3 - Use Undo Check Out to undo your changes.

In this task, you remove the stairs of the drawing and then decide to replace the drawing with the latest version in the vault by selecting **Undo Check Out** in the External References palette.

1. Remove the stairs in the drawing by selecting the stairs and pressing <Delete>.

2. Select **Yes** to check out the drawing and select **Yes** to update properties, when prompted.

3. You now decide you want to return to the version with the stairs. In the External References palette, select **WALK THROUGH**, right-click, and click **Undo Check Out**.

4. Select **Yes** to confirm that you want to replace the drawing with the latest version in the vault. Notice that the stairs are now back in the drawing.

Task 4 - View the version history in Autodesk Vault.

In this task, you view the version history in Autodesk Vault.

1. In AutoCAD, click (Autodesk Vault) in the *Vault* tab>Access panel.

2. In Autodesk Vault, click (Refresh).

3. Locate **WALK THROUGH.dwg**.

4. View the two versions in the *History* tab and note the comments, as shown in Figure 6–29.

Thumbnail	File Name	Revision	State (Historical)	Created By	Checke...	Comment
	WALK THROUGH.dwg			user1	5/10/201...	Removed fountain
	WALK THROUGH.dwg			user1	5/10/201...	First submission to Vault

History Uses Where Used Change Order Preview

Number of versions: 2 (Local = Version #2)
Number of revisions: 1   ☑ Show all versions

Figure 6–29

Practice 6b

Rolling Back an AutoCAD Design

Practice Objective

- Use the **Get** command to retrieve a previous version.

In this practice, you view the version history of a drawing in the vault. You then use the **Get** command to roll back the drawing to a previous version, since the changes in the latest version are no longer desired.

Task 1 - View the version history in Autodesk Vault.

1. In Autodesk Vault, log in as user1. Locate **Office.dwg** and view its version history in the *Preview* tab.

2. Compare the two versions of the drawing. The elevation view was removed in Version 2.

Task 2 - Get the previous version of the drawing.

In this task, you use the **Get** command to retrieve Version 1 of Office.dwg with the elevation view added.

1. In Autodesk Vault, locate and select **Office.dwg**, right-click, and then click **Check Out**.

2. Now in the *History* tab, select version 1 of **Office.dwg**, right-click, and click **Get** as shown in Figure 6–30.

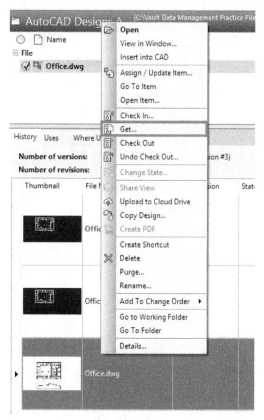

Figure 6–30

3. Click >> to expand the details of the Get dialog box.

4. Notice that it shows version 1 with the elevation view, as shown in Figure 6–31.

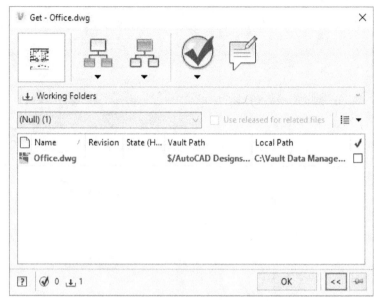

Figure 6–31

5. Click **OK** to copy the Version 1 file to your local working folder.

6. Click **Yes** when prompted to overwrite the file with data from the vault, as shown in Figure 6–32.

Figure 6–32

7. Notice that, as expected and as shown in Figure 6–33, the vault status icon changes to  (Incorrect version Refresh the file), indicating that the local file is older than the one in the vault.

Figure 6–33

Task 3 - Open a previous version in AutoCAD.

In this task, you open version 1 of **Office.dwg** into AutoCAD from the local working folder.

1. In AutoCAD, click **Open**. You are not selecting **Open from Vault**, because this time you want to retrieve the local copy of the drawing.

2. Browse to the ...\vault_work\AutoCAD Designs A folder and double-click **Office.dwg**.

3. Notice that the drawing is the version with the elevation view.

4. Open the External References palette. The vault icon has changed there as well to  (Incorrect version Refresh the file) indicating that it is older than the latest version in the vault.

5. Save the drawing and perform a Check In. Type **Rolled back to design with elevation** in the comments area, then click **OK**.

6. Close the drawing.

Task 4 - View the drawing history in Autodesk Vault.

1. In Autodesk Vault, view the version history of **Office.dwg** specifically to ensure that the latest version has the elevation view, as shown in Figure 6–34.

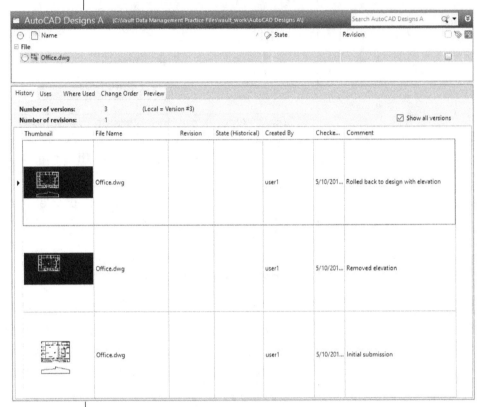

Figure 6–34

In summary, you retrieved an earlier version of the drawing, and then checked in the drawing, making it the latest version. This procedure is also known as the Leap Frog Approach.

2. Close the drawing.

Practice 6c

Releasing an AutoCAD Design

Practice Objectives

- Change the category of a file using **Change Category**.
- Change the lifecycle state and revisions of files using **Change State**.

In this practice, you will change the category of a file using the **Change Category** command and then change its lifecycle state and revision using the **Change State** command.

Typically, your files will already be assigned to a category and therefore, all that would be needed is to use the Change State command to release a file or set of files.

Task 1 - Change the category of a file.

1. In the Autodesk Vault software, log in as administrator (no password) and navigate to the $\AutoCAD Designs C folder. Notice that the files have no State or Revision listed.

2. Select **SITE SURVEY-M.dwg**, and then in the toolbar, select **Change Category**.

3. Select **Engineering**, as shown in Figure 6–35.

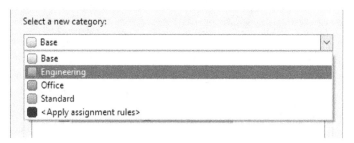

Figure 6–35

4. Click **OK**. The State now displays as **Work In Progress** with a Revision of **A**.

Task 2 - Release a file using Change State.

1. Select **SITE SURVEY-M.dwg**, right-click, and select **Change State**.

2. Select **Released** from the drop-down list. The comments automatically display *Released to manufacturing*, as shown in Figure 6–36.

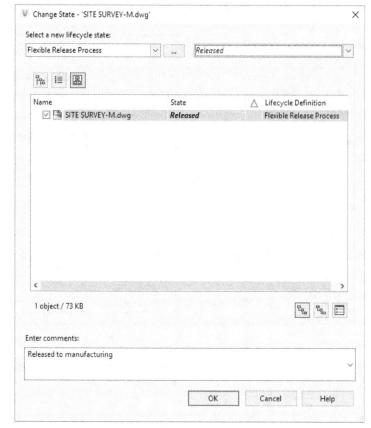

Figure 6–36

3. Click **OK**. The result displays as shown in Figure 6–37. Note that the file is still at *Revision* **A**, and the State is now set to **Released**. The file is also locked as indicated by the vault status icon.

Figure 6–37

Task 3 - Create a new revision using Change State.

1. In Autodesk Vault, select **SITE SURVEY-M.dwg**, right-click, and select **Change State**.

2. Select **Work In Progress**, as shown in Figure 6–38.

Figure 6–38

3. Click **OK**. The *Revision* changes to **B**.

4. Typically, you would now open the file in AutoCAD, check it out, make a design change and then check in the file.

Chapter Review Questions

1. A file needs to be checked out to modify it.

   a. True

   b. False

2. What are the steps for reverting to a previous version of an AutoCAD file?

   a. Use Check Out, and then open the file from the working folder.

   b. Check Out the file. In the file's *History* tab, ensure that the **Show all versions** option is selected, and then select the required version. Right-click, select **Get**, and then click **OK** to download.

   c. Use **Get**, select the previous version from the list, then use the **Open from Vault** command to open the previous version from the vault database.

   d. Use **Get**, select the previous version from the list, then open the file from the working folder.

   e. Use **Get**, select the latest version from the list, then open the file from the working folder.

3. By default, .DWF files are automatically created and attached to the files on check in.

   a. True

   b. False

4. What does the red arrows ( ) vault status icon indicate?

   a. The file is locked and the local copy is up-to-date.

   b. The local copy is a historical revision of the leading revision in the vault.

   c. The file is not in the vault. Use Check In to add the file to the vault.

   d. The local copy does not match the latest version in the vault.

Command Summary

Button	Command	Location
	Check In	• **AutoCAD Ribbon:** *Vault* tab>File Status panel • Shortcut menu in the Vault Browser
	Get	• **Menu:** Actions>Get • **Shortcut:** (*right-click on selected file*) • **Standard Toolbar**
	Check Out	• **Menu:** Actions>Check Out • **Shortcut:** (*right-click on selected file*)
	Undo Check Out	• **AutoCAD Ribbon:** *Vault* tab>File Status panel • Shortcut menu in the Vault Browser
	Change Category	• **Menu:** Actions>Change Category • **Toolbar** (Behaviors)
	Change State	• **Menu:** Actions>Change State • **Toolbar** (Behaviors) • **Shortcut:** (*right-click on selected file*)

Customizing the User Interface

You can customize the user interface of the Autodesk® Vault software to improve productivity and efficiency.

Learning Objectives in This Chapter

- Customize the Autodesk Vault interface using the View menu.
- Change the column display in the Autodesk Vault software using the **Customize View** option.
- Apply a filter to the main table using the filter options.
- Create a custom view using the Define custom views menu.
- Create a shortcut to access frequently used designs.

7.1 Autodesk Vault Customization

The **View** menu options control the display of the Autodesk Vault window. The menu is shown in Figure 7–1.

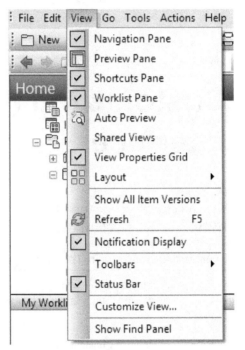

Figure 7–1

Pane Display

You can toggle the interface items shown in Figure 7–2 on and off.

Standard toolbar

Properties grid

Advanced toolbar

Navigation pane

Shortcuts pane

Preview pane

Find panel

Status bar

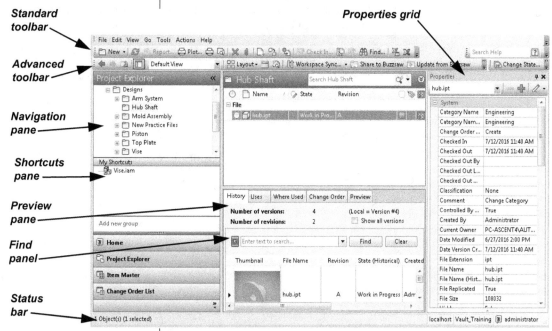

Figure 7–2

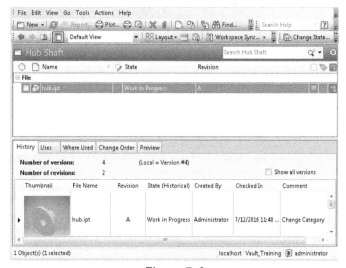 *(Preview pane) is also located in the Advanced toolbar.*

If a window pane is on (displayed), you can toggle it off (hide it) by selecting its option in the **View** menu. For example, you can toggle the Navigation pane and the Properties grid off so that the Main table and Preview pane fill the extra space, as shown in Figure 7–3.

Figure 7–3

Auto Preview

Auto Preview can also be toggled on or off in either the View menu or from the Advanced toolbar (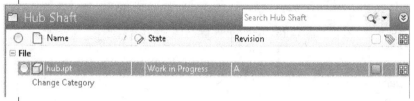). When on, objects display in the Main table with comments directly below them, as shown in Figure 7–4.

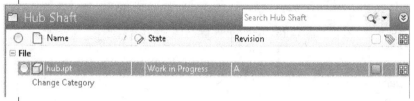

Figure 7–4

7.2 Customizing Columns

The **Customize View** option enables you to customize the column display in the Main table, Preview pane, and Search Results window. This can increase your productivity by displaying only the required file property information in an easy-to-view display.

The **Customize View** option is available when you right-click on a column heading, as shown in Figure 7–5.

*The **Customize View** option is also available when you right-click in any white space in the Main table or Preview pane.*

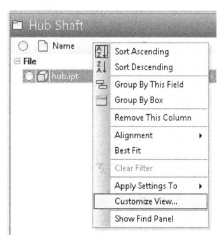

Figure 7–5

When you select **Customize View**, the Customize View dialog box opens as shown in Figure 7–6. The options available vary depending on whether you click **Customize View** in the Main table, Preview pane, and Search Results window.

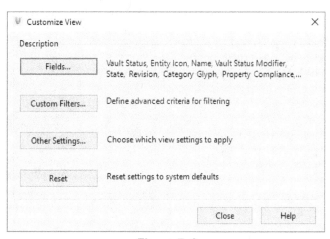

Figure 7–6

Column Display

To customize the columns that display, click **Fields...** in the Customize View dialog box. The Customize Fields dialog box opens. The *Show these fields in this order* area contains the columns that are currently displayed and their display order, as shown in Figure 7–7.

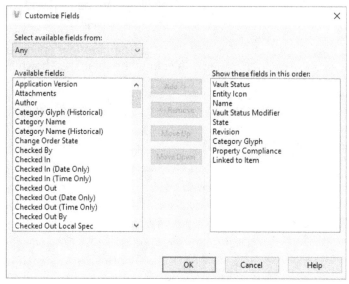

Figure 7–7

Adding Columns

You can add columns to the Main table and customize the order in which they display.

How To: Add Columns to the Main Table

1. In the Customize Fields dialog box, in the Select available fields from drop-down list, select one of the options as shown in Figure 7–8.

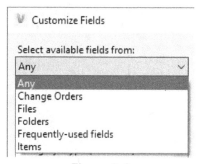

Figure 7–8

2. In the *Available fields* area, select a property as shown in Figure 7–9. Click **Add** to move the property to the *Show these fields in this order* area.

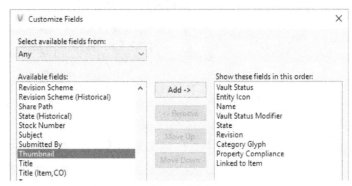

Figure 7–9

3. Click **OK**.

Changing Column Order

In the Customize Fields dialog box, the order in which the columns are shown is the order in which they display in the Main table.

How To: Change the Column Order

1. In the Customize Fields dialog box, in the *Show these fields in this order* area, select the property field to reorder.
2. Click **Move Up** to move the property field up (i.e., to the left in the Main table). Click **Move Down** to move the property field down (i.e., to the right in the Main table).
3. Click **OK**.

You can also change the column order by dragging and dropping a column heading to a new position in the Main table.

Removing Columns

You can remove columns from the Main table.

How To: Remove a Column

1. In the Customize Fields dialog box, in the *Show these fields in this order* area, select the property to remove.
2. Click **Remove**. You can also remove a column by selecting a column heading, right-clicking, and selecting **Remove This Column**.
3. Click **OK**.

Text Alignment

You can modify the alignment of the text displayed in the columns in the Main table.

How To: Align the Text in a Column

1. Select the column heading, right-click on **Alignment** to display the alignment options as shown in Figure 7–10.

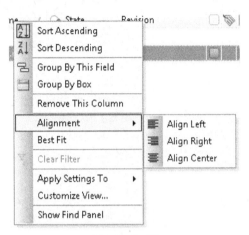

Figure 7–10

2. Select the required type of alignment: **Align Left**, **Align Right**, or **Align Center**. The text in the column updates accordingly.

Column Size

You can modify the width of the columns in the Main table.

How To: Resize a Column

1. Hover over the right edge of the column heading border so that the double arrowheads display (↔).
2. Drag the border to manually resize the column.

You can also resize columns as follows:

*   Select the column heading, right-click, and select **Best Fit** to automatically resize the column to fit the data.

*   Double-click on the right edge of the column heading border to automatically fit the column width to the data.

Sorting

You can sort the data that displays in the columns in the Main table.

How To: Sort Data in a Column

You can also select the column heading to switch between the ascending and descending sort type.

1. Select the column heading, right-click, and select **Sort Ascending** or **Sort Descending**.

   - **Sort Ascending:** Sorts columns from A to Z, reading from top to bottom (or from the lowest to highest number). If a column is sorted in ascending order, an up arrow displays in the column heading, as shown in Figure 7–11.

   - **Sort Descending:** Sorts columns from Z to A, reading from top to bottom (or from the highest to lowest number). If a column is sorted in descending order, a down arrow displays in the column heading as shown in Figure 7–12.

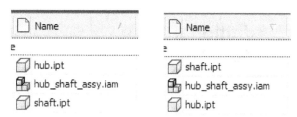

Figure 7–11   Figure 7–12

Grouping

You can sort the contents of the Main table and Preview pane by any combination of column headings. Objects that have the same values for the selected properties are then listed together. For example, you can group a folder by designer, version, date, etc. for a more manageable view of the folder.

How To: Group by Column Headings

1. Select the column heading, right-click, and select **Group By This Field**. The column heading is moved to the *Group By Box* area and the contents are grouped and collapsed, as shown in Figure 7–13.

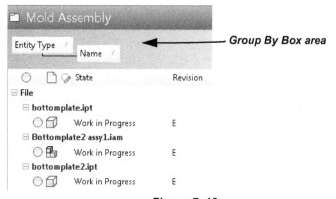

Figure 7–13

You can also drag the column heading next to the first one in the Group By Box area to add a sub-group. Drag it back to the other column headings to remove the sub-group.

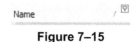 *(Group By Box) is also located in the Advanced toolbar.*

2. If you need to place another group in the first one (a sub-group), right-click on another column heading, and select **Group By This Field**.
3. To expand all of the groups, right-click in the *Group By Box* area, and select **Full Expand**.
4. To collapse all of the groups, right-click in the *Group By Box* area, and select **Full Collapse**.
5. To clear the group so that the files display as a flat list without any groups, right-click in the *Group By Box* area, and select **Clear Grouping**.
6. To remove the *Group By Box* area, right-click on a column heading, and select **Group By Box** to toggle it off.

Additional Settings

Additional settings can be found by clicking **Other Settings...** in the Customize View dialog box. The settings are shown in Figure 7–14.

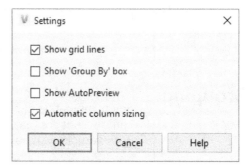

Figure 7–14

Filters

You can hide contents based on specific criteria by defining column filters.

How To: Create a Column Filter

*Filters can also be created by clicking **Custom Filters...** in the Customize View dialog box.*

1. In the Main table or Preview pane, hover the cursor over a column heading. A filter icon displays, as shown in Figure 7–15.

Name

Figure 7–15

2. Click the filter icon and select either the *Values* tab or the *Text Filters* tab, as shown in Figure 7–16.

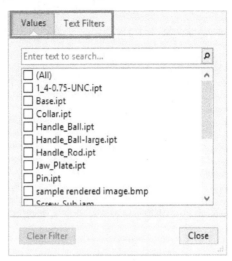

Figure 7–16

3. To create a filter from column values, in the *Values* tab, select checkboxes next to the files whose data you would like displayed, as shown in Figure 7–17. Note that the files are displayed immediately and the filter is shown at the bottom of the main table. Click **Close** when finished.

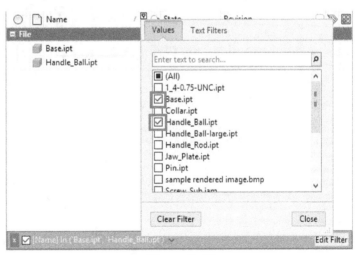

Figure 7–17

4. To create a filter using text filters, in the *Text Filters* tab, select an operator from the drop-down list, as shown in Figure 7–18.

Figure 7–18

5. Enter a value for the condition, as shown in Figure 7–19. The filtered list displays immediately. Click **Close** when finished.

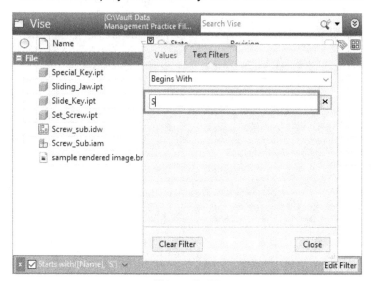

Figure 7–19

6. To create a custom filter, select the *Text Filters* tab and select **Custom Filter** in the drop-down list, as shown in Figure 7–20.

Figure 7–20

7. In the *First* search criteria section, select an operator from the drop-down list and enter a value for the condition, as shown in Figure 7–21.

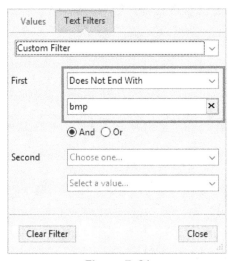

Figure 7–21

8. You can specify up to two types of search criteria. Select **And** to combine the criteria or select **Or** to contain either criteria.
9. Click **Close** to complete the custom filter definition. The line at the bottom of the pane indicates that a custom filter is being used, as shown in Figure 7–22. Click **Edit Filter** to modify the filter's definition.

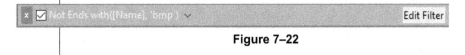

Figure 7–22

*The filter can also be removed by right-clicking on the column heading and selecting **Clear Filter**.*

10. When a filter is created, you can temporarily toggle it off or remove it. To toggle off a filter, click ☑ at the bottom of the Main table list. To remove the filter, click ☒. Toggling off or removing a filter causes the complete list of files to be displayed. Click ⌄ to select from the list of available filters.

Reset Current View

To reset the column view to the default configuration, click **Reset** in the Customize View dialog box.

7.3 Custom Views

Custom views enable you to create your own configuration of the interface. Once created, you can modify, rename, copy, delete, or reuse them.

How To: Create a Custom View

1. In the Advanced toolbar, expand the drop-down list and select **Define custom views...** as shown in Figure 7–23.

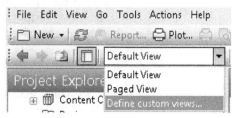

Figure 7–23

2. In the Manage Custom Views dialog box, click **New...**.
3. For *View Name*, enter a name for the custom view and click **OK**.
4. In the Manage Custom Views dialog box, click **Modify...**.
5. In the Customize View dialog box, click **Fields...**.
6. In the Customize Fields dialog box, select the columns that you want to display in the custom view.
7. Click **Close** to close the dialog box and apply the settings.

7.4 Shortcuts

Shortcuts can be used to quickly access specific folders or objects. When the shortcut is selected, the associated folder or object displays in the Main table. Vault shortcuts can also be accessed in the Autodesk Inventor Open and Place From Vault dialog boxes for quick retrieval of components and designs.

When created, shortcuts are added to the My Shortcuts pane, which is part of the Navigation pane. The My Shortcuts pane is hidden when the Navigation pane is hidden but can also be hidden independent of the Navigation pane. To hide the My Shortcuts pane, clear the **View>Shortcuts Pane** option.

Shortcuts can be renamed, organized by groups, and removed. Shortcut groups can be created to organize your shortcuts for quick and easy access.

Create Shortcut

You can create shortcuts to quickly access frequently used folders or objects.

How To: Create a Shortcut

1. In the Navigation pane or Main table, select a folder or file.
2. Right-click and select **Create Shortcut**. A shortcut displays in the My Shortcuts pane, as shown in Figure 7–24. In this example, a shortcut was created to the *Hub Shaft* folder and to the **Operating instructions.doc** file.

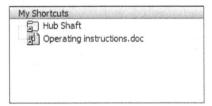

Figure 7–24

3. To rename a shortcut, right-click on it and select **Rename**. Enter a new name.
4. To remove a shortcut, right-click on it and select **Delete**. Only the shortcut is removed and not the associated folder or object.

Create Shortcut Groups

You can organize your shortcuts using groups to make them easier to locate.

How To: Create a Shortcut Group

1. In the My Shortcuts pane, right-click and select **New Group**. Enter a name for the group.
2. Drag existing shortcuts to the new group and drag them in the group to change their order. An example of a group is shown in Figure 7–25.

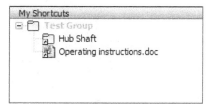

Figure 7–25

3. To rename a shortcut group, right-click on it and select **Rename**. Enter a new name.
4. To remove a shortcut group, right-click on it and select **Delete**. This also removes any shortcuts in the group.

Practice 7a

Customizing the User Interface

Practice Objectives

- Use the View menu and Customize View option to customize the Autodesk Vault window.
- Apply a filter to the main table.
- Create a shortcut.

In this practice, you will customize the user interface to display only the Main table and thumbnail images in the Main table. You will also use a filter to hide .GIF files in the Main table and add a frequently accessed assembly to the Shortcut pane.

Task 1 - Toggle off the Navigation and Preview panes.

In this task, you will toggle off the Navigation and Preview panes so that only the Main table displays.

1. In the Autodesk Vault software, select the *AutoCAD Designs A* folder.

2. Select **View>Navigation Pane** and **View>Preview Pane** so that these panes are no longer displayed.

Task 2 - Add a new column field to the Main table.

In this task, you will add a new column to the Main table so that you can display a thumbnail image.

1. In the Main table, right-click on a column heading and select **Customize View**.

2. In the Customize View dialog box, click **Fields...**.

3. In the Customize Fields dialog box, expand the Select available fields from drop-down list, and select **Files**.

4. In the *Available fields* area, select **Thumbnail** and click **Add** to add it to the *Show these fields in this order* area.

5. In the *Show these fields in this order* area, select **Thumbnail** and click **Move Up** so that it is first in the list. Click **OK**.

6. Click **Close** to close the Customize View dialog box and complete the change. The thumbnail images display in the first column for each applicable file in the Main table, as shown in Figure 7–26.

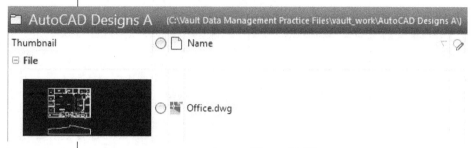

Figure 7–26

Task 3 - Adjust the Name column.

Double-click on the border on the right side of the *Name* column heading to adjust the column size to fit the data.

Task 4 - Apply a filter to the Main table.

In this task, you will create a custom filter to exclude all .GIF files from the display.

1. Select **View>Navigation Pane** to display the Navigation pane.

2. Select the *AutoCAD Designs B* folder.

3. Identify the *logo.gif* file. This is the file that you will filter out of the display.

4. Hover the cursor over the *Name* column and click ⬙.

5. Select the *Text Filters* tab.

6. In the *Text Filters* tab, select **Custom Filter** in the drop-down list, as shown in Figure 7–27.

Figure 7–27

7. Select the **Does Not End With** operator. For the condition, type **gif**, as shown in Figure 7–28.

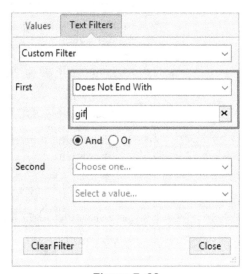

Figure 7–28

Once a filter is created, it is available for use in all folders.

8. Click **Close**. The .GIF file is removed from the display and the filter displays at the bottom of the pane, as shown in Figure 7–29. You can disable the filter by clearing the checkmark.

Figure 7–29

Task 5 - Undo/delete the customizations.

In this task, you will undo the user interface customizations.

1. Select **View>Preview Pane** to toggle on the Preview pane.

2. To delete the thumbnail image from the Main table, select the Thumbnail column heading, right-click, and select **Remove This Column**.

3. Click  at the bottom of the Main table to remove the filter and see the *logo.gif* file return to the list.

Task 6 - Add a shortcut.

In the *AutoCAD Designs A* folder, select **Office.dwg**, right-click, and select **Create Shortcut** to add the assembly to the My Shortcuts pane, as shown in Figure 7–30. You can also drag the file to the My Shortcuts pane. If the My Shortcuts pane is not displayed, click **View>Shortcuts Pane**.

My Shortcuts
Office.dwg

Figure 7–30

Chapter Review Questions

1. In the Autodesk Vault interface, what are some of the ways in which you can customize the window display? (Select all that apply.)

   a. You can toggle on and off the Navigation and Preview panes.

   b. You can apply a filter to a column to only display objects with specified file formats, for example.

   c. You can change the font size in the main table.

   d. You can resize and reorder the columns.

2. How can you resize columns to fit the data? (Select all that apply.)

   a. Drag the border to manually resize the column.

   b. Select the column heading, right-click, and select **Alignment**.

   c. Select the column heading, right-click, and select **Best Fit** to automatically resize the column to fit the data.

   d. Double-click on the right edge of the column heading border to automatically fit the column width to the data.

3. How do you remove a filter? (Select all that apply.)

   a. Click at the bottom of the Main table list next to the filter.

   b. Select the column heading, right-click, and select **Clear Filter**.

   c. Click at the bottom of the Main table list to place a checkmark for the filter.

   d. Click **Reset** in the Customize View dialog box.

4. When you remove a shortcut, you also remove the associated folder or object?

   a. True

   b. False

Command Summary

Button	Command	Location
	Auto Preview	• Advanced Toolbar
	Group By Box	• Advanced Toolbar
	Preview Pane	• Advanced Toolbar

Chapter 8

File and Design Management

One of the Autodesk® Vault software's key features is its ability to consolidate and manage all product information for easy reference, sharing, and reuse. In this chapter, you learn about managing files in the vault, editing object properties, and the Copy Design tool. The Copy Design tool copies an entire design, including all related files, while maintaining their relationships to each other in the new design file.

Learning Objectives in This Chapter

- Use the Move, Delete, and Attachments operations to move, delete, and attach files to other files in the vault.
- Use the Edit Properties operation to edit object properties.
- Create a label to capture a project milestone.
- Use the Rename operation to rename files and update all related files that reference the renamed files.
- Use the Replace operation to replace files with new files and update the parent references.
- Use the **Pack and Go** command to copy all referenced files to a single location outside the AutoCAD software.
- Use Workspace Sync to clean up files in your project workspace.
- Use the Copy Design operation to create a new design.

8.1 Managing Data in the Vault

Autodesk Vault's data management functionality includes the ability to move, delete, rename, and attach files to other files in the vault.

Required for Autodesk Inventor Files

To ensure file resolution when performing data management operations on Autodesk Inventor files, the project specified in Autodesk Inventor's Project Settings is used. An administrator can set up an Autodesk Inventor project file to be used for all of the clients. If you are not an administrator, you can specify the Autodesk Inventor project file in the Autodesk Vault software by selecting **Tools>Options** or by right-clicking on the project file and selecting **Set Inventor Project File,** as shown in Figure 8–1.

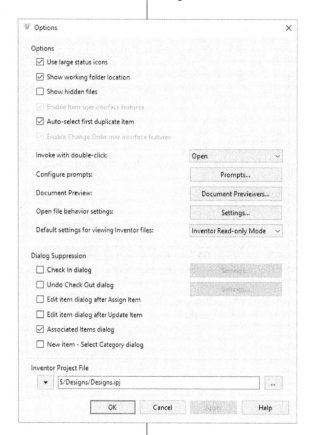

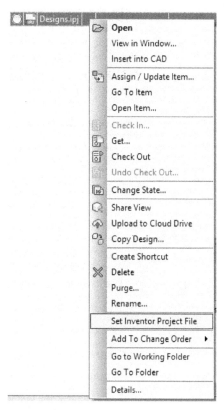

Figure 8–1

Moving Files

You can also move a file by dragging and dropping it into its new folder using the left mouse button.

To move files from one folder to another, select the files in the Main table, hold the right mouse button, and drag them into the target folder. When you release the right mouse button after dragging, select **Move** as shown in Figure 8–2.

Figure 8–2

The file remains the same in the new location and is still referenced by its children and parents.

Deleting Files

To delete vault files, select them in the Main table, right-click, and select **Delete**. You are prompted to confirm the action. The **Delete** operation deletes all versions of the selected files. You can also delete files by clicking ✕ (Delete) in the Main toolbar or selecting **Edit>Delete**.

When using the **Delete** operation:

- Parents need to be deleted before children.

- A file must be in a **Checked In** state.

- If a file label exists, it needs to be deleted before the file is deleted.

Attaching Files to Other Files

Files can be attached to other files in the vault, which creates a link between the files so that they act as a unit when being checked out and checked in. For example, you might want to attach a Microsoft Word document containing operating instructions to a design file.

How To: Attach a File to Another File

1. In the Main table, select the files to which you want to attach a file and select **Actions>Attachments**.
2. Click **Attach...** and select the files to attach.
3. Click **OK**.

Attachments display with a paper clip symbol, in the *Uses* tab, as shown for **yoke.ipt** in Figure 8–3.

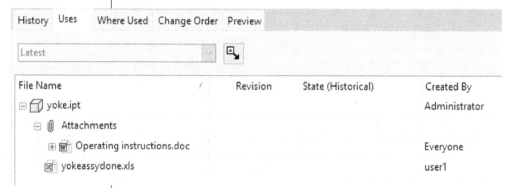

Figure 8–3

How To: Remove Attachments from a File

1. In the Main table, select the file from which you want to remove an attachment and select **Actions>Attachments**.
2. Select the attachment filename and click **Detach**.
3. Click **OK**.

8.2 Properties

Editing Properties

The Autodesk Vault software includes both System-Defined Properties and User-Defined Properties (UDPs). The **Edit Properties** command in the Autodesk Vault software enables you to edit User-Defined Properties of selected objects, such as files, items, and change orders. When updating file properties, files are automatically checked out and then checked back in to the vault with the file property updates.

How To: Edit File Properties

Your user role must be defined as Editor or Administrator to edit file properties. Items can only be edited by an Item Editor Level 1, Item Editor Level 2, or an Administrator.

You can also select multiple object types for editing.

1. In the Autodesk Vault software main table view, with the objects selected, select **Edit>Edit Properties**. Alternatively, with the objects selected, in the Properties grid, click

   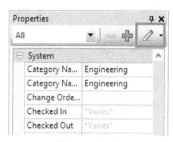 (Edit Properties), as shown in Figure 8–4.

Figure 8–4

2. The Property Edit dialog box opens displaying the objects to edit. You can add additional objects or remove any objects using **Add** and **Remove**, respectively. By default, the properties of **Name**, **Author**, and **Description** display.
   - Properties that display with a gray background are read-only.
   - Properties that display with a white background can be edited. Double-click the property and type a new value.

3. Click (Select Properties) to add more properties.
4. In the Customize Fields dialog box, in the *Select available fields from* drop-down list, select one of the following options to determine the type of properties to be displayed: **All fields**, **Files**, **Folders**, or **Frequently-used fields**.
5. In the *Available fields* area, select a property.
6. Click **Add** to add the property to the *Show these fields in this order* area.
7. In the *Show these fields in this order* area, use **Move Up** or **Move Down** to organize the properties.

The new value for a file property must be the appropriate data type or it displays as incorrect.

8. In the *Show these fields in this order* area, use **Remove** to remove a property from the list.
9. Click **OK**.
10. Edit the properties by double-clicking on a cell and changing its value. You can also right-click on a cell to access the **Copy**, **Paste**, **Select All**, **Capitalize**, **Find**, and **Replace** options, as shown in Figure 8–5.

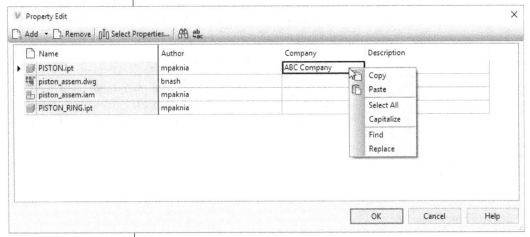

Figure 8–5

11. Drag the small black square at the bottom right corner of the selected cell to fill the other cells with the same value.
12. Click **OK**.
13. The Property Edit Results dialog box opens displaying the updated properties as shown in Figure 8–6.

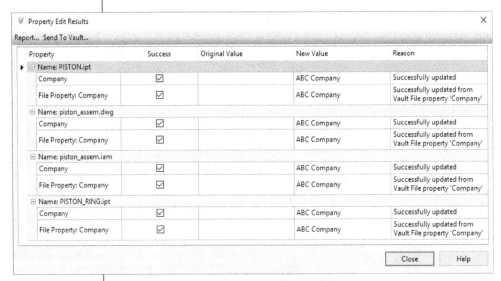

Figure 8–6

14. Select **Report** to print or export the results. The Preview window enables you to use the following options to modify, print, or export the report:

    - Add a header or footer, adjust the margins, and set the display to **Portrait** or **Landscape**.
    - Add a watermark or change the color of the background.
    - Export the report as a .PDF, .HTML, .MHT, .RTF, .XLS, .XLSX, .CSV, .TXT, or image file.
    - Send the report via email.
    - Customize how the report is going to print by selecting which items are going to print (header, footer, lines, etc.) and how the report is going to fit on the printed page.

15. In the Property Edits Results dialog box, select **Send To Vault** to save the report in the vault. In the Save As dialog box, select the vault in which to save the report, enter the report name, and click **Save**.

16. Click **Close**. The *Comment* field displays **Property Edit** to explain the version change for files with modified properties.

Creating UDPs

How To: Create a New User-Defined Property

1. Click **Tools>Administration>Vault Settings**.
2. Select the *Behaviors* tab and click **Properties**.
3. In the Property Definitions dialog box, click **New**.
4. In the New Property dialog box, enter a name.
5. In the Type drop-down list, select the property type, as shown in Figure 8–7.

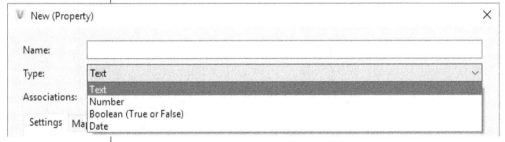

Figure 8–7

6. Assign the UDP to one or more categories by selecting the category checkboxes in the Associations drop-down list, as shown in Figure 8–8.

- Categories can be preselected in this list based on the filter you selected previously in the Property Definitions dialog box.
- You can select or clear categories as required.

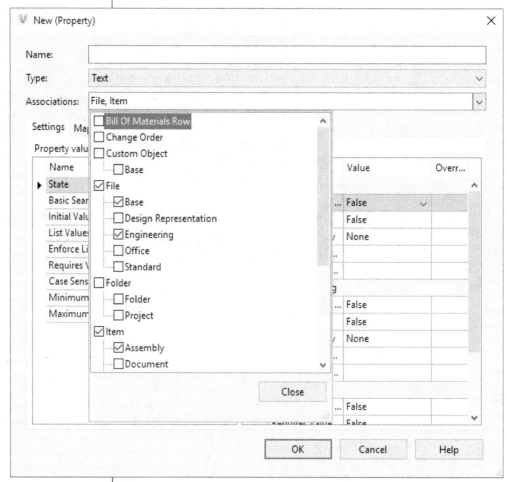

Figure 8–8

Add or Remove Properties

How To: Add or Remove Properties from Files or Items

1. Select the required objects and then select **Actions>Add or Remove Property**.
2. Locate the property and select **Add** or **Remove** from the Action drop-down list, as shown in Figure 8–9.

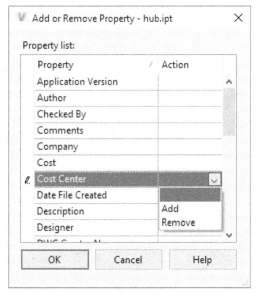

Figure 8–9

8.3 Labels

In the Autodesk Vault software, labels can be created to capture project milestones, such as customer proposals and design reviews. They act as snapshots of your data at a specific point in the design process. You can assign specific documents to these labels. Once the label has been created, you can use the **Pack and Go** operation to create a package based on that label. You can also roll back the design based on a label.

How To: Create a Label

1. Select **Tools>Labels**. The Labels dialog box opens as shown in Figure 8–10.

Figure 8–10

The Labels dialog box displays the list of labels that have already been defined and enables labels to be created, deleted, renamed, archived, and restored. It displays the *Created By* and *Create Date* information on a label, the number of files assigned to it, and any associated comments.

*You can also create a new label by selecting a vault folder, right-clicking, and selecting **New Label**.*

2. In the Labels dialog box, click **New...** to create a new label. The New Label dialog box opens as shown in Figure 8–11.

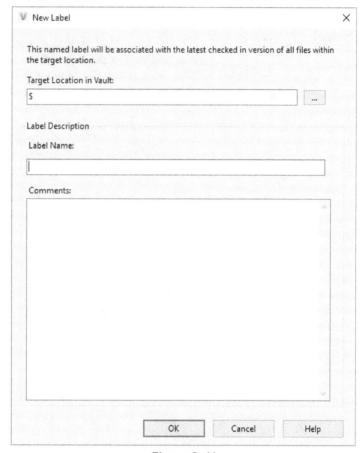

Figure 8–11

There is no limit to the number of labels that can be assigned to a project.

*Label names must be unique in the database and can contain any alphanumeric text, excluding \ / : * ? " < > |*

3. Select the target location for the label. The latest version of all of the files at that location is assigned that label. If child references exist outside the specified location, those files are also assigned that label.

4. Enter the name of the label that indicates the milestone. Since the folder information is not included, it is a good idea to include it in the name.

5. Enter comments that clearly summarize the content of the label.

6. Click **OK**.

Editing a Label

To edit a label, select one from the list and click **Edit...**. Enter a new name or edit the comments and click **OK**.

Deleting a Label

To delete a label, select a label from the list and click **Delete**. Click **Yes** to confirm deletion.

Extracting a Label

To extract a label, select a label from the list and click **Pack and Go** to create a package of the label contents. Specify the Pack and Go details, as shown in Figure 8–12, including selecting which label to retrieve.

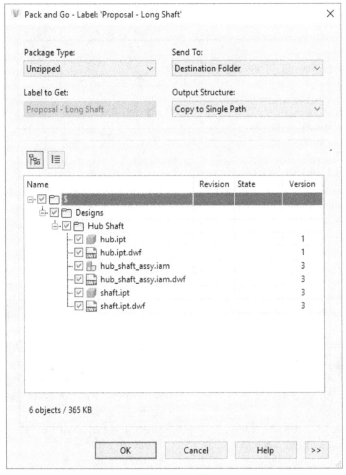

Figure 8–12

Restoring

When restoring a label, the version of the file associated to the label becomes the current version. To restore a label, select one from the list and click **Restore**. Click **Yes** to confirm the restore and creation of the new version.

8.4 Rename Wizard

Your user role must be defined as Editor or Administrator to use the Rename Wizard.

The **Rename** operation in the Autodesk Vault software uses the Rename Wizard. In addition to renaming files, this operation updates all related files that reference the renamed files to ensure that all relationships remain intact. You must have permission to check out the files. Any file in the vault can be renamed using the Rename Wizard, except for .DWF files which are automatically published.

How To: Use the Rename Wizard

You can also select a file and then select Edit>Rename.

1. In the Autodesk Vault software, select the files, right-click, and select **Rename**. The Rename Wizard opens listing the files to be renamed and their vault folders. You can add or remove files in this page.
2. Click **Next>**. The Rename Wizard dialog box displays all related files and their vault locations that are affected by the name change.
3. Click **Next>**. Enter the new name for each file in the list, as shown in Figure 8–13.

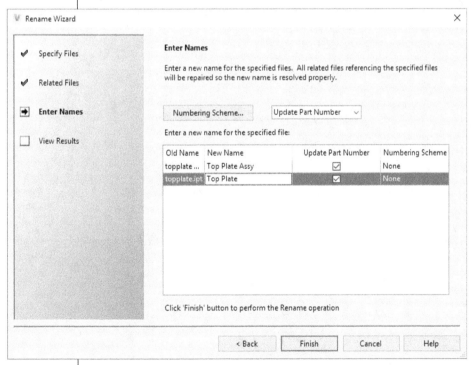

Figure 8–13

4. Select the checkbox in the *Update Part Number* column if you want to assign the new filename to the Part Number iProperty for Autodesk Inventor files.
5. Click **Finish**. The Rename Wizard performs the operation and displays the results.
6. Click **Save...** to export the results. Select the folder in which to save the report, enter the report name, and click **Save...**
7. Click **Send to Vault...** to save the report in the vault. Select the vault in which to save the report, enter the report name, and click **Save...**.
8. Click **Close**.

8.5 Replace Wizard

The Replace Wizard enables you to replace files with new files, which automatically updates the parent references. A new version of the parent that references the new file is created.

How To: Use the Replace Wizard

1. In the Autodesk Vault software, select the files, and select **Edit>Replace**. The Replace Wizard dialog box opens listing the files to be replaced and their vault folders. You can add or remove files from this page.
2. Click **Next>**.
3. In the Related Files page, all parent files display by default. To exclude a parent file from being updated with the new reference, clear the associated option.
4. Click **Next>**.
5. In the Specify Replacement Files page shown in Figure 8–14, click 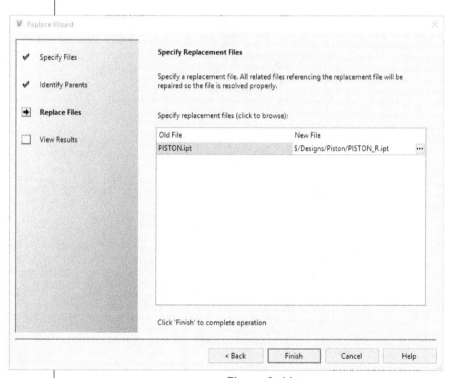 (Browse) to select a new file to replace the old file. Do this for each listed file.

Replace can also be accomplished using the ***Copy Design*** *option.*

The status of the new file that replaces the old file does not matter.

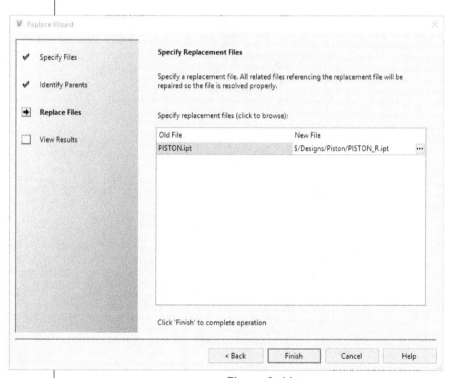

Figure 8–14

---

6. Click **Finish**. The Replace Wizard performs the operation and displays the results.
7. Click **Save...** to export the results to a text file.
8. Click **Save...** to save the report in the vault as shown in Figure 8–15. Select the vault in which to save the report, enter the report name, and click **Save...**.

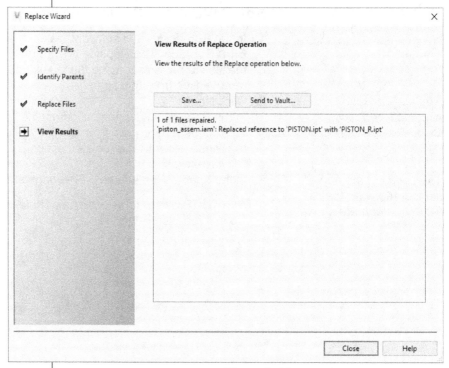

Figure 8–15

9. Click **Close**.

8.6 Pack and Go

An AutoCAD drawing can reference multiple files. The **Pack and Go** tool enables you to copy all of the referenced files to a single location outside of the AutoCAD software, while also maintaining links to the referenced files.

The **Pack and Go** tool is useful for archiving files, isolating a design for experimentation, and providing a complete project to a vendor who might not have access to the Autodesk Vault software.

How To: Package a File and Its References in Autodesk Vault

1. In the Autodesk Vault software, select the file that you want to package.
2. Select **File>Pack and Go**. All of the files referenced by the selected file display as shown in Figure 8–16.

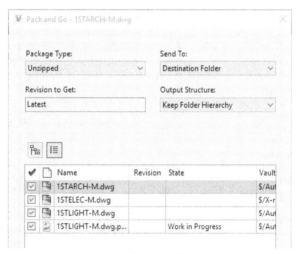

Figure 8–16

3. Set the *Package Type* option to one of the following:
   - **Zip file (*.zip)**
   - **Unzipped**
   - **DWF Package**
   - **DWFx Package**
4. Set the *Send To* option to one of the following:
   - **Destination Folder**
   - **Mail Recipient**
   - **SharePoint Directory**

5. Set the *Revision to Get* option to the revision you want to package (**Latest**).
6. Set the *Output Structure* option to one of the following:
   - **Copy to Single Path**
   - **Keep Folder Hierarchy**

7. Click 🖳 (Settings). In the Settings dialog box, in the *Children (uses)* and *Other relationships* areas, select one of the following options:
   - **Include dependents**
   - **Include attachments**
   - **Include library files**
   - **Include related documentation**

8. In the Settings dialog box, in the *Visualization Filter* area, select one of the following options:
   - **Include Visualization Files**
   - **Exclude Visualization Files**
   - **Visualization Files Only**

9. Click [>>] if you would like to append a transmittal report to the package. Select the **Append transmittal report to package** option and a template file, as shown in Figure 8–17.

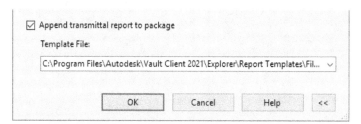

Figure 8–17

10. Click **OK**. If **Mail Recipient** was selected in the *Send To* field, an email message opens. Depending on the Package Type selected, you are prompted for a folder or filename.

8.7 Synchronize Your Workspace

You can synchronize the contents of your local workspace with the corresponding Vault folders. This operation either updates the files in either location, or removes files from the workspace.

You can click **Workspace Sync** to manually select the local files to synchronize and select the Settings for additional options. Alternatively, you can select **Quick Sync** from the drop-down menu to synchronize immediately using the default settings.

How To: Synchronize Your Workspace

1. Select **Workspace Sync** from the toolbar, as shown in Figure 8–18.

Figure 8–18

2. Select the checkboxes for the files you would like to synchronize, as shown in Figure 8–19. Removed files are placed in the Windows Recycle Bin.

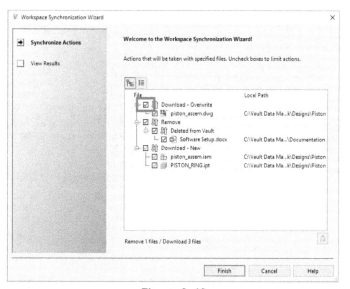

Figure 8–19

---

3. Select **Finish**. The results display as shown in Figure 8–20.

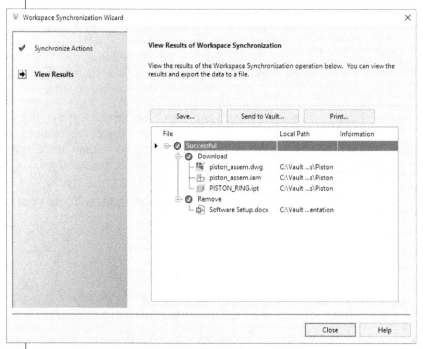

Figure 8–20

4. If you would like to save the results to a .CSV file, click **Save** to save the file to a specified folder, or click **Send to Vault** to save the file to a Vault folder. An example of a .CSV file is shown in Figure 8–21.

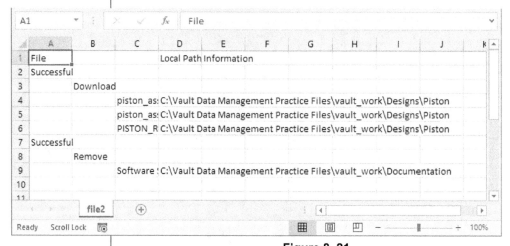

Figure 8–21

8.8 Copy Design

The **Copy Design** command enables you to copy an entire design (including all related files, parts, drawings, subassemblies, and attachments), and maintain their relationships to the new design. **Copy Design** commands can include copying, reusing, replacing, and excluding specified files from the existing design to create the new design.

Accessing Copy Design

Copy Design can be executed in Autodesk Vault using the **Edit** menu or from the right-click menu. The Copy Design interface is launched in a modeless dialog, therefore, allowing you to perform work within Autodesk Vault while performing a Copy Design. Copy Design can also be executed as a standalone application from the Windows Start menu.

Copy Design Interface

There are three major sections of the Copy Design interface: the Menu and toolbars, main view, and Navigation panel, as shown in Figure 8–22.

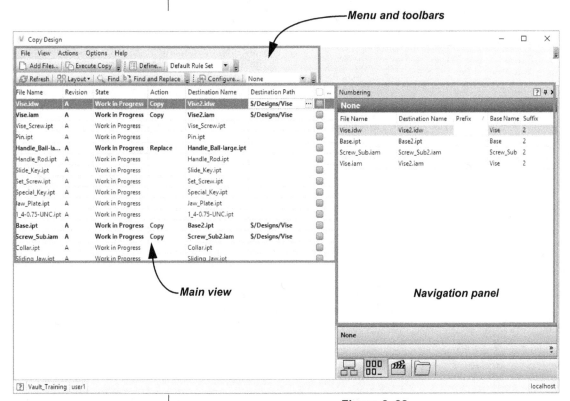

Figure 8–22

Menu and Toolbars

The Menu includes the following menus: **File**, **View**, **Actions**, **Options**, and **Help**. Many of the commands found in these menus are also found in the toolbars and context (right-click) menus.

The toolbars can be used to add files to the main view, find and replace files, control copy settings or action rule sets, and create copies. The toolbar commands are described in the table below.

Command	Description
Log In/Log Out	If Copy Design is started from the Start menu, select **Log In**, to log in to a vault to access designs for copying. Use **Log Out** to log out of a vault when you are finished or when you want to switch to a different vault.
Add Files	Add the files that you want to copy to the main view with **Add Files**.
Execute Copy	Once everything is configured, select **Execute Copy** to begin the copy operation.
Select Rule Set	A Rule set determines the file properties and settings for copied files when certain conditions are met. Users can select from a list of existing rule sets. The Rule Set sub-menu lists all of the existing rule sets. If no rule set is selected, the target file receives the same file properties and settings as the source file.
Refresh	Use Refresh to see the most recent changes to files or the design structure in the main view.
Layout	Use Layout to control the view of the files in the main view. There are three options: **Show Tree View**, **Show List View**, and **Show Folder View**.
Find/Find and Replace	Use Find to search for words or characters; Use Find and Replace to search for words or characters and replace them with the ones you want (This is handy when you want to replace all instances of a word). You can perform the operation in the main window or the numbering panel.
Configure	Enables you to configure the Numbering Scheme.

The Main View Grid

The main Copy Design view shows the name of the files available to copy, destination folder, the action that will be performed on the file, the revision and state of the file, and how many instances (Count) of the file occur in the current list.

Tip: By default, reference file names are set to the destination file name when an action is assigned. You can view the Numbering Panel to identify files by their original name, or add File Name (Historical) to the main view. You can also manage copy actions and customize the view, including filtering columns, from the main view, as shown in Figure 8–23.

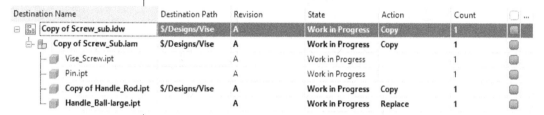

Destination Name	Destination Path	Revision	State	Action	Count	
Copy of Screw_sub.idw	$/Designs/Vise	A	Work in Progress	Copy	1	
Copy of Screw_Sub.iam	$/Designs/Vise	A	Work in Progress	Copy	1	
Vise_Screw.ipt		A	Work in Progress		1	
Pin.ipt		A	Work in Progress		1	
Copy of Handle_Rod.ipt	$/Designs/Vise	A	Work in Progress	Copy	1	
Handle_Ball-large.ipt		A	Work in Progress	Replace	1	

Figure 8–23

To change a copy action, select the file, right-click and select **Copy, Copy To..., Replace..., Exclude** or **Reuse. Copy To...** and **Replace...** prompt you to select the destination folder and replacement file, respectively.

The available file actions depend on the type of file selected. These are described as follows:

Action	Description
Copy	Generates a new file that is independent of the selected source file.
Copy To...	Enables you to change the destination folder of the selected file.
Reuse	Keeps the selected file in the new design while maintaining all links.
Exclude	Omits the selected file from the new design.
Replace...	Enables you to substitute the selected file with another one.

The Navigation Panel

There are four different navigation panels, each located on their own tab:

- Where Used

- Actions

- Numbering

- Folders

The Actions panel displays with its tab selected, as shown in Figure 8–24.

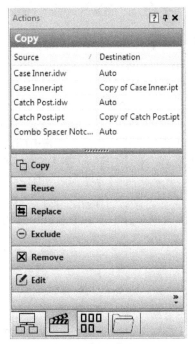

Figure 8–24

The options available in the four navigation panels are as follows:

Panel	Details
Where Used	The Where Used panel lets users track the origin of the copy objects and their destination.
	Since you can replace existing files with uncommitted instances of files that are being copied, this means that the copied instance can have numerous destinations. Use the *Where Used* tab to ensure that the files are copied to the correct locations.
Actions	The Actions panel enables you to review which operations are going to be performed on files in the main view.
	Once you have configured the files in the main view, you can use the Actions Panel to filter the files based on their assigned operation. Assigned operations include copied, reused, replaced, excluded, or edited.
	Use the Actions Panel to verify the copy design configuration in the main view and to make changes.
	Note that you can also set Action operations by dragging and dropping files from the main grid onto the required operation button in the Actions Panel.
Numbering	The Numbering Panel lists all of the files selected for copying. It also shows the original and new name for each selected file.
	The grid displays the renaming options based on available numbering schemes.
	In the Numbering Panel grid, you can edit certain fields and individual numbering schemes.
Folders	The Folders Panel enables you to review the source and destination folders for the copy design operation. This helps you verify that the required files are selected and are being copied to the correct location.
	You can group selected files for operations based on the folder location. You can also drag-and-drop files between folders or from the main grid to perform a copy. You can also display the files in a Tree View or List View. There is **Find and Replace** functionality in the List View, in the shortcut menu, as shown below.

Grid View	▶
View	▶
Choose Columns...	
Find and Replace...	
Refresh	

Performing a Copy Design

How To: Perform a Copy Design

1. Select and right-click on a file from the main table and then select **Copy Design**.
2. Select **Options** from the menu and select which of the following options do you want enabled:
   - Select References
   - Automatically Copy Parents
   - Link Drawings and Model
   - Remove BOM Object
   - Select References

   Notes: You can also access Action Rules and Numbering Schemes from this menu or from the toolbars.

3. Select **Add Files** to select the files that you want to copy and then click **Open**. The files are added to the main view of the Copy Design dialog.
4. Select **View** from the menu and select **Show Children** to select **Attachments**, **Library Files**, or both in the copy design view.
   When using Show Drawing View, view the files in Tree View by selecting **View>Layout>Show Tree View.**

5. By default, associated drawings receive the same copy action as the associated file and is denoted by a value of Auto in the Action column. In Model View, documentation set to Auto takes the same name as the dependent file being replaced or copied. This can result in file name duplication. Select **View>Show Drawing View** to turn on the Drawing View to help resolve file naming conflicts.

*Click **Refresh** to display the latest version of the listed files.*

6. If you want to perform a different action on a file, right-click on the file and select the action from the context menu.
7. In the toolbar, select the rule set from the drop-down list that you want to apply to the copy operation. The file properties and behavior settings determined by the rule set are applied to the destination files.

To apply a numbering scheme, select a numbering scheme from the button list in the Numbering panel.

8. To review the settings before executing the copy, display the **Actions**, **Folders**, **Numbering** and **Where Used** panels under **View>Panels**. View each panel and confirm all settings are correct.
9. Once everything is configured, select **Execute Copy** from the toolbar or from the **File** menu to start the copy operation.

All successful copy operations receive a green checkmark in the main view. If a copy operation failed, a red cross displays. To perform another copy operation, modify your settings and click **Execute Copy**.

Practice 8a

Data Management and Rename Wizard

Practice Objectives

- Use the Move operation.
- Attach one file to another.
- Rename an assembly and a part.

In this practice, you will use Autodesk Vault's file management functionality to move and rename files. In addition, you will attach a file to another file to have them behave as one unit.

Task 1 - Move a file from one folder to another.

1. In the Main table of the Autodesk Vault software, in the $\AutoCAD Designs B folder, locate **1STARCH-M.dwg**.

2. View the drawing's details in both the *Uses* and *Where Used* tabs, as shown in Figure 8–25, noting its XREF and where it is used.

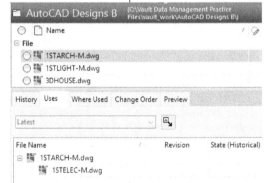 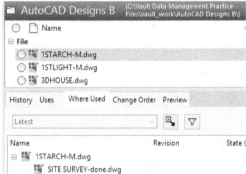

Figure 8–25

3. In the Main table, select **1STARCH-M.dwg** and drag it into the $\AutoCAD Designs C folder in the Navigation pane.

4. In the $\AutoCAD Designs C folder, select **1STARCH-M.dwg**. In the Preview pane, select the *Uses* and *Where Used* tabs to see that it maintains the parent and child relationships.

Task 2 - Attach one file to another.

In this task, you will attach a Microsoft Word document to an AutoCAD file so that they behave as one unit when checking out and checking in.

1. Select **1STARCH-M.dwg**.

2. Select **Actions>Attachments**.

3. In the Attachments dialog box, click **Attach...**.

4. In the Select File to Attach dialog box, in the $>*Documentation* folder, locate and select the file **Operating instructions.doc**. Click **Open**.

5. In the Attachments dialog box, click **OK**.

6. In the Preview pane, select the *Uses* tab. Note that the Attachments node contains an entry, as shown in Figure 8–26.

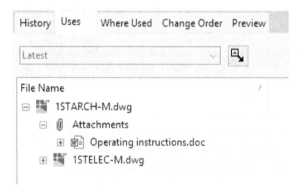

Figure 8–26

Task 3 - Rename an assembly and a part.

In this task, you will use the Rename Wizard to rename **1STARCH-M.dwg**.

1. In Autodesk Vault, browse to the *$\AutoCAD Designs C* folder, if you are not already there.

2. Select **1STARCH-M.dwg**, right-click, and select **Rename**. The Rename Wizard opens as shown in Figure 8–27.

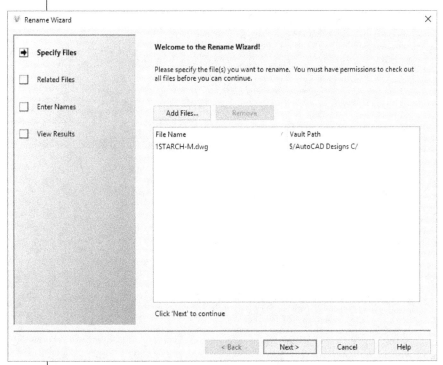

Figure 8–27

3. Click **Next>** to continue. There are no files affected by the rename so the Related Files page was automatically skipped.

4. Enter a new name for the file, as shown in Figure 8–28.

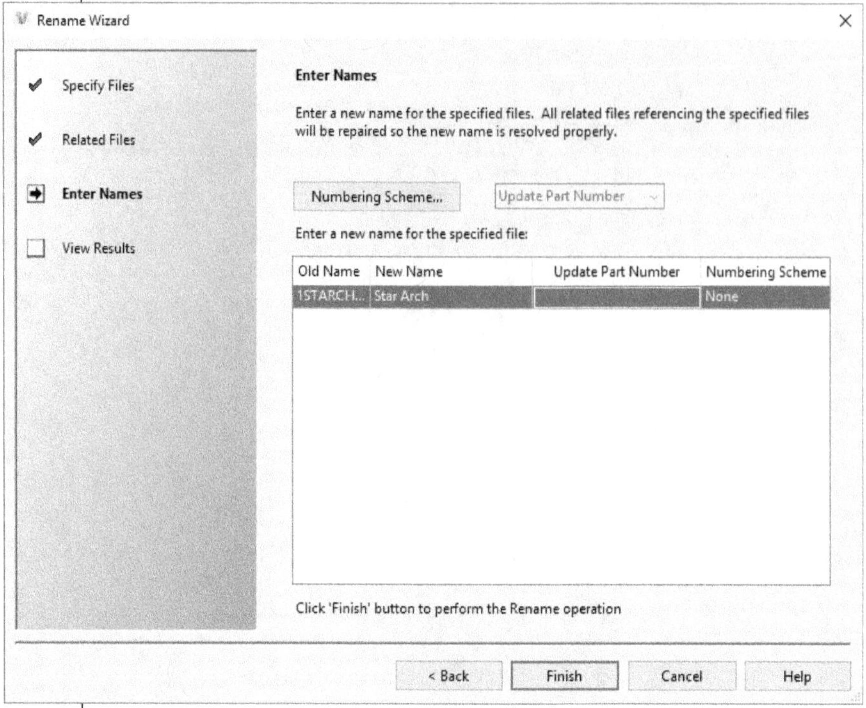

Figure 8–28

5. Click **Finish**.

6. Click **Send to Vault...** to save the report in the vault. Locate the *...\Documentation* folder and name the file **Renaming Report**. Click **Save**.

7. In the View Results page, confirm that both renames were successful, including the part number updates, as shown in Figure 8–29.

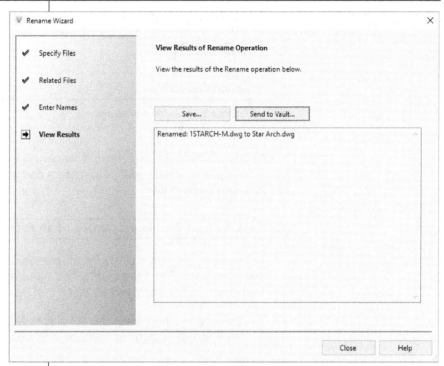

Figure 8–29

8. Click **Close**.

9. In the Main table, select **Star Arch.dwg**. In the Preview pane, select the *History* tab. The **Rename** operation has created Version 3 of the file and the comments have been filled in automatically, as shown in Figure 8–30.

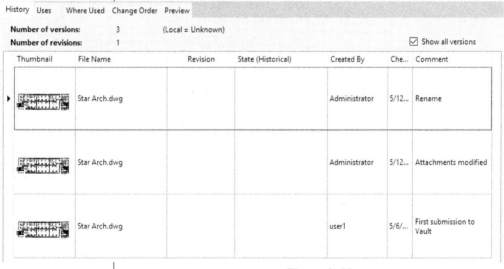

History   Uses   Where Used   Change Order   Preview

Number of versions: 3   (Local = Unknown)
Number of revisions: 1   ☑ Show all versions

Thumbnail	File Name	Revision	State (Historical)	Created By	Che...	Comment
	Star Arch.dwg			Administrator	5/12...	Rename
	Star Arch.dwg			Administrator	5/12...	Attachments modified
	Star Arch.dwg			user1	5/6/...	First submission to Vault

Figure 8–30

Practice 8b

Editing File Properties and Labeling

Practice Objectives

- Edit the file properties of an assembly.
- Create a label.

In this practice, you will edit file properties in the Autodesk Vault interface and create a label to mark a design milestone for the hub shaft assembly.

Task 1 - Edit the file properties of an assembly.

In this task, you will edit the file properties of an assembly and two of its parts. The file property that requires editing, **Company**, first needs to be displayed so that it can be edited.

1. Select all of the files in the $\Designs\HubShaft folder (**hub_shaft_assy.iam**, **hub.ipt**, and **shaft.ipt**) and, in the

   Properties grid, click (Edit Properties).

2. Click (Select Properties) to customize the list of file properties to edit.

3. Expand the Select available fields from drop-down list and select **Files**.

4. Select **Company** and click **Add** to add it to the list of file properties to edit.

5. Move **Company** so that it displays after **Author** in the list and click **OK**.

6. Double-click in the *Company* cell for the file in the first row. Enter **ABC Company** and press <Enter>. Drag the small black box in the bottom right corner of the cell to copy the value to the other *Company* cells, as shown in Figure 8–31.

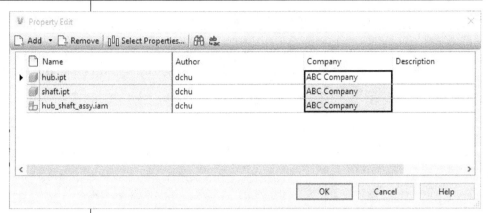

Figure 8–31

7. Click **OK**.

8. The Property Edit Results window opens displaying the results with the new **Company** value, as shown in Figure 8–32.

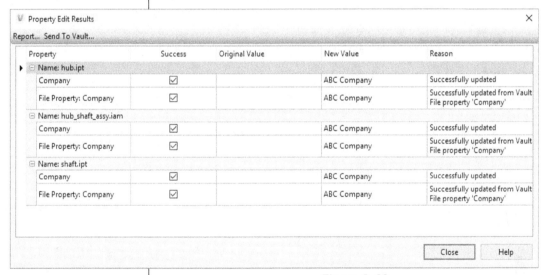

Figure 8–32

9. Select **Send To Vault** to save the report in the vault. Navigate to the *$\Documentation* folder and name the file **New Company Report**. Click **Save**.

10. Click **Close**.

Task 2 - Create a label.

In this task, you will create a label to mark a proposal milestone that displays the hub shaft design with a longer shaft.

1. Select **Tools>Labels**.

2. Click **New...** to create a new label.

3. The New Label dialog box opens. For the target location, click 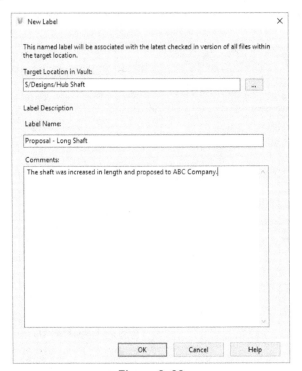 (Browse). Expand the *$\Designs* folder and select the *Hub Shaft* subfolder. Click **OK**.

4. For the label name, enter **Proposal - Long Shaft**.

5. In the *Comments* area, enter **The shaft was increased in length and proposed to ABC Company.**, as shown in Figure 8–33.

Figure 8–33

6. Click **OK**. In the Labels dialog box, the details of the new label display.

7. Click **Close** to close the Labels dialog box.

Practice 8c

Copy Design

Practice Objective

- Create a new design using the **Copy Design** command.

In this practice, you will make a copy of **SITE SURVEY-done.dwg** using the **Copy Design** command.

Task 1 - Start the Copy Design process.

In this task, you start the **Copy Design** command and select the files you want to copy, reuse, and replace.

If you need to remove all files from the dialog box, select the root node, right-click, and select **Clear Root Node**.

1. In the Main table, right-click on **SITE SURVEY-done.dwg** and select **Copy Design**.

2. To display the files in a list, select **View>Layout>Show Tree View**.

3. Using <Ctrl>, select files **SITE SURVEY-done.dwg** and **LANDSCAPE PLAN-M.dwg**, then right-click and select **Copy**.

4. Select **ASCENT logo.gif**, right-click, and select **Replace**. Navigate to the *AutoCAD Designs B* folder, select **logo.gif**, and click **Replace**. The Copy Design window displays as shown in Figure 8–34.

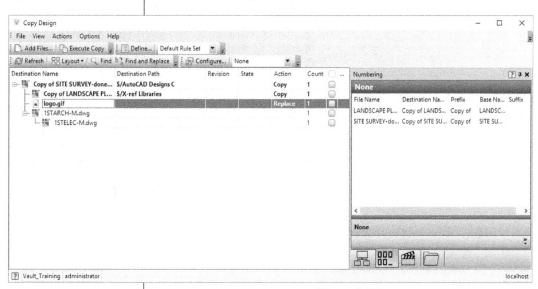

Figure 8–34

If the Numbering panel is not displayed, select View>Panels> Numbering.

5. In the *Numbering* panel on the right, right-click in the background and select **Set Values** to set values for both the *Prefix* and *Suffix*. Remove the value for *Prefix* and enter **2** for *Suffix*, as shown in Figure 8–35.

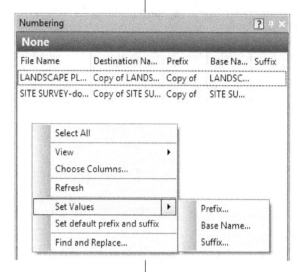

Figure 8–35

6. The *Destination Name* column values update as shown in Figure 8–36.

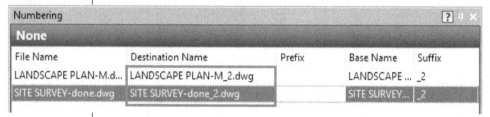

Figure 8–36

7. In the Main View, click in the *Destination Path* field for **SITE SURVEY-done_2.dwg**, and then click ⋯ and create a new folder under *$* named *AutoCAD Copied Designs*. The Destination Path is updated, as shown in Figure 8–37.

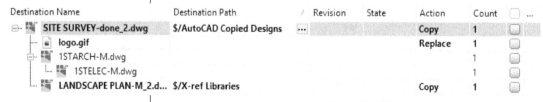

Figure 8–37

Task 2 - Create a copy of the files and view the copied files.

In this task, you will execute the Copy Design operation of the selected files.

1. Click **Execute Copy** in the toolbar to start the copy operation. When successful, a green checkmark will display for the **Copy** and **Replace** actions, as shown in Figure 8–38.

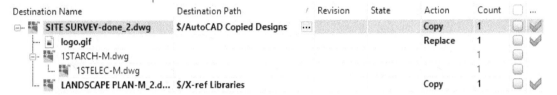

Destination Name	Destination Path		Revision	State	Action	Count		
SITE SURVEY-done_2.dwg	$/AutoCAD Copied Designs	...			Copy	1	☐	✓
logo.gif					Replace	1	☐	✓
1STARCH-M.dwg						1	☐	
1STELEC-M.dwg						1	☐	
LANDSCAPE PLAN-M_2.d...	$/X-ref Libraries				Copy	1	☐	✓

Figure 8–38

2. Close the Copy Design window. In the Autodesk Vault client, browse to the *AutoCAD Copied Designs* folder to view the copied **SITE SURVEY-done_2.dwg** file and view the *Uses* tab to view the files used in the copied file, as shown in Figure 8–39.

Figure 8–39

Task 3 - Open the Vise2 assembly.

In this task, you will open the Vise2 assembly.

1. Select **Vise2.iam**, right-click, and select **Open** to open it in the Autodesk Inventor software. Click **No** to when prompted to check out the assembly.

2. In the Vault Browser, verify that **Vise2.iam** references **Base2.ipt**, **Screw_Sub2.iam**, and **Handle_Ball-large.ipt** are under **Screw_Sub2.iam**.

Chapter Review Questions

1. When you move a file from one location to another, the file effectively remains the same in the new location and is still referenced by its children and parents.

   a. True

   b. False

2. What do you need to remember when using the **Delete** operation? (Select all that apply.)

   a. Parents need to be deleted before children.

   b. Children need to be deleted before parents.

   c. A file must be in a **Checked In** state.

   d. If a file label exists, it needs to be deleted before the file is deleted.

3. When a label has been created, which operation is used to create a package based on that label?

   a. Edit

   b. Copy Design

   c. Pack and Go

   d. Restore

4. When files are attached to other files in the vault, a link is created between the files so that they act as a single unit when they are checked out or checked in.

   a. True

   b. False

5. When using **Copy Design**, what operations can be performed on the files? (Select all that apply.)

   a. Copy

   b. Reuse

   c. Exclude

   d. Replace

Command Summary

Button	Command	Location
⬚	Select Properties	• Property Edit dialog box

Index

www.ingramcontent.com/pod-product-compliance
Lightning Source LLC
LaVergne TN
LVHW062312060326
832902LV00013B/2163